Beyond
a mere
Christianity

Beyond a mere Christianity

Fran Rogers

"But God hath revealed them unto us by his Spirit:
for the Spirit searcheth all things,
yea, the deep things of God."
1 Corinthians 2:10

Beyond a mere Christianity

1st Edition
© 2019 Fran Rogers
Father and Family Books

ISBN–13-978-1732681439

All rights reserved

godsgracegodsglory.com

Scripture quotations are from the Holy Bible KJV
in public domain.
Strong's Concordance references from blueletterbible.org.

Cover by Mithun

Dedication

This book is dedicated to Bill Sweeney and Terri Nida whose testimonies are included. They are proof that a mere Christianity is not enough for living in the wilderness of this world. They witness of God's grace that goes beyond what we can ask or imagine, and their witness has given hope to thousands of others.

Acknowledgements

Many thanks are due to my WordPress readers and others who follow my blog. Encouragements came throughout the year as we published each chapter. Bruce Cooper was a blessing as a beta reader with excellent feedback. And as usual, Jerry, my husband, is my most ardent supporter.

CONTENTS

Introduction

1. Many Religions 13
2. Inexhaustible Goodness 17
3. The Need for a True Christianity 21
4. God is Here 25
5. I Cannot Write Fast Enough 31
6. Weakness and Meekness 35
7. Control or Solutions 39
8. The New Nature of a True Christian 43
9. Endear and Endure 47
10. Three Powerful Words 51
11. The Right Man for the Job 57
12. A Holy, High, and Heavenly Calling 59
13. Covenant Living and Giving 65
14. Seeing IS Believing 69
15. How Exciting is Your God? 73
16. Good Works 77
17. Peace and Contentment 85
18. Breakthrough and Follow-Through 91
19. Bound by Grace ~ Free to Love 95
20. God's Utmost for My Highest 105
21. Focus, Love, and Rejoice 109
22. Living Sacrifices 113
23. Abiding in Light and Truth 119
24. Preaching, Teaching and Reaching 123
25. What is Jesus Doing in Your Life? 127
26. Riveted and Radical 137
27. Nailing Our Thesis 143
28. The Secret Place 147
29. Striving and Surviving 157
30. Thriving in Enemy Territory 165
31. Arrows in the Hands of a Mighty King 177
32. The Shaft of Faith 189

33. Living by Faith 199
34. More Life in His Kingdom 213
35. Conclusion to a *mere* Christianity 217
36. Unshakable Hope 221
37. Everything for His Glory and our Good 225
From the Author 229

Introduction

When I began this series on my WordPress blog in June 2018, I did not know if it would be a book. Like Abram, not foreseeing what the end would be, I started with faith that the Lord was leading and blessing the process for me to seek His will, His instructions, and His provisions. He continues to reveal amazing things of His kingdom. Even as I write this introduction, it is with knowledge I did not have a year ago. This treatise is meant to challenge us to take what we have received from all sources He has given over the years, to seek, and grow stronger in our faith. Most of the valuable works for the kingdom are by men who are no longer living but the Lord still lives to lead us beyond what we have already—so as to be hungry for more than men can give us. I want to continue on this course with joy and excitement to publish as many books as He wills for me. I had hoped to publish this one by my eightieth birthday on August 1 but decided to settle down and enjoy how the Lord would bring this to pass in His own timing. Every day in obedience, there is communion and fellowship with Him as He continues to *show me His ways, teach me His paths, and lead me in His truth—for He is the God of my salvation, and I wait on Him all day* (Psalm 25:5).

Why the title *Beyond a Mere Christianity*? C. S. Lewis' book *Mere Christianity* was the first of the two other books and a sermon that came to mind when I posted the list of chapters for this series. I use each of these regarding the Christian faith of men who have died but whose works are still speaking to people today. After reading and studying these books by C. S. Lewis, Francis Schaeffer, Oswald Chambers, and Jonathan Edwards' sermon, I retained the main things they taught. The Lord used each one to bring me to a greater knowledge of Him.

Though I have lived longer than these men, I can never know all they knew. But the Lord has challenged me during every decade to seek more and more of His kingdom through a committed and vibrant relationship with Him—to look further than what I learn from men.

He sits as our great High Priest, with the promise and power of the Holy Spirit, to teach us from His Holy Word. The more time we spend with Him personally in prayer and the study of His Word, the more powerful our Christian faith becomes. From generation to generation, we can all learn and share with others.

Meaning of the Word *Mere*
One definition of mere is *pure, simple,* being nothing more than specified. Another definition for mere is *a small pond of standing water.* *Vocabulary.com*

This latter meaning has become intriguing in the use of the word as a noun; *mere—a lake; a shallow body of water.* This definition lends itself to the meaning of this book. Christianity is thought by some to be shallow—*as a small pond of standing water.* Such thoughts negate the moving of the Holy Spirit and the depth of His working in the hearts and lives of God's people.

In a synonym study, Dictionary.com compares the words *mere* and *bare,* which implies a scant sufficiency. They are often interchangeable, but *mere* frequently means no more than (enough). Thus, a *mere* livelihood means enough to live on but no more; a *bare* livelihood means scarcely enough to live on.

So, when I hear the title *Mere Christianity*, it seems from my former understanding to mean that Christianity is nothing more than any other religion. When we try to make Christianity a common faith, we are in danger of dumbing down the power that Christ died to give us. We lose the essence of the faith that is by grace alone, the working of the Holy Spirit for the revelation of the truths of God's Word.

Many, by reading Lewis' book, are encouraged to embrace Christianity even as he did. I believe God has used His work to bring many to a knowledge they never had and who have become followers of Christ. My purpose in writing is to look beyond what he believed, spoke, and wrote, to discover a greater depth, beyond a *mere* Christianity; for a *mere* Christianity will not suffice for Christ's followers to proclaim and to live the legacy God has bestowed on His children. We will see this in the testimony of Bill and Terri.

How Lewis Used the Word *Mere*

Lewis may have used the word *mere* to express the Christian faith as *pure* and *simple*. It is *pure*. It is *simple* and needs nothing added for those who embrace Christ and who live by the power of the Holy Spirit.

But to those who do not know Him, Christianity is a complex, misunderstood faith. It is much, much more to those who are growing in the doctrines of the faith. It is a living faith—a powerful faith beyond any others. It is a way of life to those who are being transformed by the power of the teachings of Jesus Christ and the Word of God—The Holy Bible.

When the gospel is watered down so as to satisfy everybody, we withhold the wealth that comes only by a personal relationship with the Father and Jesus, His Son. Christianity comes at a high price, the blood of Jesus Christ.

To receive the inheritance that is ours in Christ is a supernatural act of the Holy Spirit working through new hearts, drawn to and committed to Him. His grace does not relieve us of duty, but binds us to it and fulfills the requirement, whereby we experience this new life, a heavenly life above and beyond what most people know.

Others have written from Lewis' theme but with a different perspective. In the following chapters, we will incorporate many facets of the kingdom that our heavenly Father reveals to us, through His Word and His Holy Spirit, in and through the life of His Son, Jesus Christ.

Through these, we pray He will make clear His role as a loving heavenly Father, Creator, Redeemer, and our Life; His presence and power, His name, His kingdom, and His will.

These are His truths, promises, and blessings for a people who know Him, fear Him, love Him, obey, worship, serve, praise, pray, proclaim, and live in the power of the good news of Christ. They are for those who are being transformed as living sacrifices and conformed to His image, bearing the fruit of love, joy, peace, long-suffering, gentleness, goodness, faith, meekness and temperance, holiness, righteousness, truth, grace, humility and compassion.

This is to live the "abundant life" (John 10:10) in the "fulness of God" Ephesians 3:19), "Christ in you, the hope of glory" (Colossians 1:27) here in this life, as He continues to prepare us for eternity with Him. True Christianity is separate from any other religion—and the reality of a holy life in union with our heavenly Father and our Lord and Savior, Jesus Christ, by the power of His Holy Spirit. (This needs repeating.)

To us and in us, He reveals Himself as Jehovah, the Lord our God. He sires children of His own as His image-bearers. Though not perfect, we are His offspring through His Son, as He continues to lead us through an imperfect world, shining through us His holiness and humility.

He calls us to discover *the deep things of God*. He leads us to more than floating or possibly a casual swim in a shallow pond. He brings us to the ocean's edge and directs us to "Launch out into the deep."

Gracious and glorious Father, continue to lead us in the paths of righteousness, leaving our shallow thoughts of you to plunge the depths of your grace, your love, your presence and power—to live the abundant life to which you call us in Christ. In Jesus' name, I pray. Amen. Fran 9/2019

1

Many Religions

There are many religions—religions for the body, religions for the mind, religions for the spirit and soul—of man. Nations form their own religions. Children are born and grow up in their family religions.

We live by what we learn from others. Everyone has a religion, even if they cannot express it verbally. The mind of every person is a tablet, written on from their birth into this world.

In my autobiography, I express my birth as if being given a coloring book and a set of crayons. At every age and stage, a new coloring book and a new set of crayons were presented. My mind, heart and spirit took in everything I saw, heard, and experienced, so as to live accordingly. What I read and learned became my religion. My parents or S. S. teacher gave me a Bible, so I learned what I read there sporadically, from sermons in church, Sunday School, and vacation Bible school.

The principles were taught in our home, but not verbatim. The golden rule was prevalent, with a general understanding of right from wrong, but not Biblically profound. Neither my parents nor I understood anything beyond what we could see and touch, although I had a sense of something more. We pursued nothing that we could not easily understand. They accepted difficult times as normal, with only dim hopes of improvement in this life. "When We All Get to Heaven" was the favorite hymn sung in church, with the accompanying of a "hellfire and brimstone" sermon.

Christianity, far beyond anything I learned in my childhood, is a powerful act of God's grace that overtook, overcame, and still overrides everything in this life. It is not man's religion but from heaven; from God, revealing Himself as Creator and Redeemer of humanity. He reveals His plans, His work, His presence, His power, and His sovereignty in the writings of the Holy Bible. These are all more than the normal scope of human wisdom and living.

If we read casually, we will find a crumb or two of the religion we are looking for. If we study hard and often, diligently seeking something to believe and live by, we may see some difference in our lives. We may even sense a religion to share with others. We may worship with others of the same faith, but it is still only man's religion. It is nominal or what we think of as normal Christianity.

It is what the world sees, and a view that colors God and the church with only a slightly different tone than the world's colors.

Mere living is below the standards of God's kingdom. It is settling for the world's goods. It is negating the faith given from and in a living God to settle for man's ideas of life.

In the chapters ahead, let us leave these thoughts of man's mere faith and look heavenward to the Lord, our God and the only true religion of which He is the focus.

Our Lord Jesus is the center, and the Holy Spirit among us and within us, is directing all things according to the will of the Father. By His grace, He shows us a higher plane on which to dwell.

Father in heaven, our Lord and God, we thank you for all that you are, more than we can ask or think; for our Lord, Jesus, and for your Holy Spirit. We praise you for your Word, the truth of your Word, the authority of your Word, the glory of your Word—your Living Word, Jesus Christ, commanded in us by the power of your Holy Spirit. Speak to our hearts as you dwell within us.

Make us aware through your Word, written and living within us, of something more than men have told us. Give us a deeper understanding of who you are, so we know whose we are—that we may continue to proclaim the legacy of your kingdom of grace—to your glory and our joy. In Jesus' name, we pray. Amen.

2

Inexhaustible Goodness

When I rest in what I think I know of God, I become weary. If I depend on words I have learned of His kingdom and glory, I soon realize that, like Peter on the mount of transfiguration, there is nothing I can do for Him.

In a staggering momentum I try to keep up with His thoughts and ways, until the years of providence show me there is no holding, resting, or keeping up with Jehovah, the God who created and maintains the heavens and the earth. Words cannot convey the magnitude of His being and working. Knowledge is only the beckoning that draws us to Him, so we can live in wonder and awe of His magnificent glory as God, the Creator and Redeemer of mankind. Even with all that His Word says, we can never get our hearts and minds around His inexhaustible goodness.

His Goodness in the Old Testament

Strong's concordance for *goodness* in Hebrew translates: 2617 *achased,* lovingkindness 2896b *tob,* a good thing, benefit, welfare 2898 *tub,* good things, goods

Think of a *tub* overflowing with all that our heavenly Father desires to give His children—better still, our languishing in His goodness. When we study Psalm 107, we see that of the nation of Israel, God's chosen people, not many knew Him, yet He continued to bless them and provide for them.

In His goodness, He gave instructions; through His law, He promised blessings and curses similar to those He gave Adam and Eve—but written so that there would be no doubt as to their meanings and consequences. In rebellion, without His counsel, they were afflicted; he *therefore brought down their heart with labour; they fell and there was none to help* (vs. 12).

Then, *they cried unto the Lord in their trouble, and he saved them out of their distresses* (6,13,19,28)   .

Four times in this Psalm, we read of their rebellion, crying out to God, and His saving them. Each of these is followed by the same statement.

> "Oh that men would praise the Lord for his goodness, and for his wonderful works to the children of men!" (8,15,21,31).

We are to be grateful that His goodness does not depend on us, but only on Him. We do not know of His goodness except through our needs, and in those needs, He pours out an abundance of His goodness to us, never-ending because He is always good.

His goodness is a facet of His glory; what we cannot see visibly, we see spiritually in His provisions to us as His children, both physical and spiritual.

In Exodus 34:6, Moses asked God to reveal His glory to him,

> "And the Lord passed by before him, and proclaimed, The Lord, The Lord God, merciful and gracious, longsuffering, and abundant in goodness and truth,"

He promises His goodness to those who fear and trust in Him (Psalm 31:19).

> "I had fainted, unless I had believed to see the goodness of the Lord in the land of the living." Psalm 27:13

"The earth is full of the goodness of the Lord." Psalm 33:5

"Surely goodness and mercy shall follow me all the days of my life: and I will dwell in the house of the Lord for ever." Psalm 23:6

His Goodness in the New Testament
Goodness in Greek translates: 2570 *kilos,* beautiful, good 19 *agathosune,* virtue, beneficence

In Romans 2:4, we read that His goodness leads us to repentance.

"Or despisest thou the riches of his goodness and forbearance and longsuffering; not knowing that the goodness of God leadeth thee to repentance?" Romans 2:4

Goodness is listed as a *fruit of the Spirit,* the nature and disposition of Christ, working in and through us by His Spirit. Goodness is related to God's love, the first of the fruit listed in Galatians 5:22. His desire for us is that we bear His image, a work that only He can reveal through the power of His Holy Spirit in us. We can read and believe that we are His children through a spiritual birth, but we can never on our own bring this to pass. Read and try as we might, we soon learn that all of life is a mystery we can never explain here and now. In faith, we continue to *seek His kingdom and His righteousness,* while He is doing His Holy work in us.

"He is bountiful and gracious, ready to do them good, and He is the felicitating (*the means and the*) end, or the blessedness of the soul. The goodness of God to His creatures, according to different respects to them, has its different and various appellations. As it is freely bestowed, it is grace; as it respects them as needy, it is bounty; as it respects them in misery, it is mercy and compassion; as it respects them as provoking, so it is patience; as it intends their good, it is love; as it answers both their necessities and capacities, it is all-sufficiency."

All these—His bounty, mercy, compassion, patience, love, and all-sufficiency—are, in a word, His goodness; and goodness calls for love." *Heaven Opened - The Riches of God's Covenant* Richard Alleine [1]

Our eternal God and heavenly Father; We praise you for the overwhelming love revealed in and through Jesus Christ, your Son. We thank you for this great goodness revealed to us and in us by your Holy Spirit. Let us not settle for less than the goodness you promise, even though it is more than we can comprehend. We long for, pray, and wait for you to work it in us. Let us not lose our hope in Christ, nor grow weary, but trust you to keep us close and grow us in grace and the knowledge of our Lord Jesus Christ. In His name we pray. Amen.

---

[1] *Heaven Opened by Richard Alleine is public domain*

3

The Need for a True Christianity

In this chapter, I think of how far we have come from the corruption that ruled the church in the century of Martin Luther and other reformers. Though the church will never be perfect here in this world, we do have God's Word available for every person who desires to know the truth, so we are not depending on man for the knowledge of our relationship with God.

"Stop the world; I want to get off" is an expression from past decades which reflect the thoughts of many who wonder where the world is going.

We have enough wickedness in the world. I can't bear to see it in God's house. Having experienced eight decades of this wilderness, I think of the song *Leaving on a Jet Plane* and sometimes think I want to take that plane home to be with the Lord. Yet even as Jesus, I have a purpose here for now. We praise the Lord that He, as our Lord God Almighty, is still and always reigning and ruling over His universe. We are still learning to live in the language of a future world order with Christ as King and to spread this vocabulary wherever we can. Others need to hear and know that this world is not all there is. We will look briefly at why Christianity is necessary in the world in every generation.

What we advocate is not what is normally seen but what is real in the true Christian life and the difference we make, being who we are in Christ. We see this in the individual life and the life of the true church. We see the difference between Christianity and other religions.

The True Christian Life

Christians are those who individually and adamantly follow Jesus Christ, learning, knowing, believing and loving with all the heart, soul, mind and strength the Lord and Master who lived and died sacrificially for His people. We follow and obey Him through a knowledge of His Word, and by His Holy Spirit, we live daily by His example. This world is not our home. We are only here to witness of Him and the salvation He came to give. This life is preparation for eternity with Him and our heavenly Father in their kingdom.

The true church is not the visible church that meets every week but the invisible body of Christ whom He has brought to Himself, living where we are in every generation with others who join in worship around His Holy Word and His Supper renewing faith and love. From this gathering, we go into the world as salt, light, a sweet fragrance and full of His Spirit bearing the fruit of His kingdom—**love, joy, peace, long-suffering, gentleness, goodness, faith, meekness, temperance, holiness, righteousness, truth, grace, humility, godliness, mercy and compassion.**

True Christianity is revealed to the senses of sight, hearing, taste, smell and touch.

Salt was necessary in Jesus' day to preserve food. Salt is needful in a world that is in decay.

Light is necessary in the darkness of this world, as we "hold forth the word of life."

> "That ye may be blameless and harmless, the sons of God, without rebuke, in the midst of a crooked and perverse nation, among whom ye shine as *lights in the world*; *Holding forth the word of life*;" Philippians 2:15-16

Good fruit is produced in the life of a genuine Christian.

The Need for a True Christianity

> "Even so every good tree bringeth forth good fruit; but a corrupt tree bringeth forth evil fruit." Matthew 7:17

Fragrance is needful to cover the stench of this world's evil.

> "And we know that we are of God, and the whole world lieth in wickedness." 1 John 5:19

The world needs Jesus' touch.

> "And Jesus came and touched them, and said, Arise, and be not afraid." Matthew 17:7

The world filled and overflowing with oppression, sin, and corruption has no recourse in other religions, nor in a false Christianity. Only a true Christianity has the answer to sin through the only person who has claimed to be God and became a sacrifice for the sins of those who believe His claim on their lives.

We live, proclaiming LIFE over death. If we die for our faith, it will not be to take other lives with us, but to witness of the life of Christ **who loved us and gave His life to deliver us from this evil age** (Galatians 1:4).

We must know who we are in Christ and live accordingly. True Christianity makes a difference.

Gracious Father, we could say so much more, but you have said it all. It is but for us to read your Word faithfully, intentionally seeking your guidance for us as your people. Enable us to speak your truth wherever you lead us, living our faith to the fullest and most fruitful with our families, in our churches, and in the workplace. Shine your light in and through us into the darkness of this world. In Jesus' name, I pray. Amen.

4

God is Here

To quote directly from Francis Schaeffer's book, *The God Who Is There,* I would have to read it again. Time does not permit, so I took these notes from the Publisher's Description.

> "More than ever, The God Who Is There demonstrates how historic Christianity can fearlessly confront the competing philosophies of the world. The God who has always been there continues to provide the anchor of truth and the power of love to meet the world's deepest problems."

It is from this last sentence that I use the title, *GOD is Here,* in relation to the overall meaning of Schaeffer's book.

While Schaeffer was revealing the shift in Christianity, due to philosophy, science, history and the arts, my purpose is not to address the gainsayers, but those who follow Christ and desire a greater zeal for God and the Christian life.

The article *GOD is More* was leading to this series of articles on our blog to pique the interest of those who read His Word, yet do not really know the greatness of His power in the heart and life. The only degree that qualifies me to write in this fashion is a DDC (devoted disciple of Christ). Knowing GOD is here has been a humbling experience over decades of need, searching, studying, in meditation of God's Word, memorization, and personal encounters with a living God who is not just ruling and reigning in heaven. From His throne in heaven, He is revealing Himself to His creatures and is continually present with each one.

To speak of these things is beyond my expertise and knowledge, but with prayer, I write simply of how God has revealed Himself to me through His Word, His Holy Spirit and His presence and power in Jerry's and my life. I quote Andrew Murray, who at times apologized for not spending more time editing his work; "The Lord loves to use the feeble for His glory." *Waiting on God*

We will present this chapter in three parts:
WHO GOD IS
HOW HE IS HERE
WHY HE IS HERE

WHO GOD IS
From my childhood, there is no memory of anyone speaking of any God, except the one revealed in the Holy Bible. There is only one name of the God of Christianity. He is the LORD GOD, Jehovah, or Yahweh in Hebrew.

> "For though there be that are called gods, whether in heaven or in earth, (as there be gods many, and lords many,) But to us there is but one God, the Father, of whom are all things, and we in him; and one Lord Jesus Christ, by whom are all things, and we by him." 1 Corinthians 8:5-6

Paul speaks of the necessity for spiritual understanding apart from man's natural comprehension (Corinthians 2:9-16). We will expand on this in the second part.

Let us look briefly at who God is from His Word, remembering that He is more than we can know and understand. We grow in our conception and the reality of who and where He is through continual study and meditation. We pray and wait in faith and anticipation, desiring with all our hearts for Him to reveal Himself.

GOD our CREATOR

Our core belief is in the GOD who is our Creator. We will not waste space to debate philosophers, scientists, and historians. Genesis 1:1 is an emphatic declaration of His role as Creator of the heavens and the earth. We may not fully understand how He created and how we are individually a part of His creation but by faith we take Him at His Word. Believing means that we start with that truth, move on, read more, pray for His Holy Spirit to work faith and truth in our hearts and minds and live according to what we read. This means we must put away any pre-conceived ideas if we come across a contradiction to what we have heard before.

Christianity is not an Old Testament reality but rather, the fulfillment of Old Testament prophecy.

We base Christianity, not on how men define it, but how Jesus Christ, *the way, the truth and life* of the Christian faith, taught and lived it. John 1:1-5 speaks of Jesus being *in the beginning as The Word. The Word was with God and was God.* He was the fulfillment of Genesis 3:15, a promise of redemption for a fallen and rebellious people.

Rather than going into all the different names and characteristics of our GOD, we will look at the mainstream of His being. Christ, the Son of God, was in the beginning, for the purpose of fulfilling the prophecy of man's redemption.

GOD, our REDEEMER

> "Thus saith the Lord the King of Israel, and his redeemer the Lord of hosts; I am the first, and I am the last; and beside me there is no God." Isaiah 44:6

Other references in the Old Testament reveal that Jesus, being the Son of God, in the beginning with Him, was in an active role of redemption before His incarnation.

The LORD God, as creator and redeemer—Isaiah 44:24

The LORD God, redeemer, the Holy One of Israel—Isaiah 46:17

The LORD thy Saviour and thy Redeemer, the mighty One of Jacob—Isaiah 49:26

GOD, our FATHER

In Jesus' life and teachings, He revealed GOD as His and our heavenly Father. His disciples carried forth this most profound truth of Christianity through the early church's foundation. The supernatural work of His Holy Spirit produces a new heart and spirit (Ezekiel 36:26), a regenerating work beyond man's capacity to produce, or to reason. Our heavenly Father desired children to share the wealth of His love and glory and sires them, according to His own choosing, to inherit His eternal kingdom. Living in faith and hope of this legacy is more than a mere passing thought, but an assurance, as we serve our Father and our Lord Jesus Christ in His kingdom now.

As we have mentioned, He is much more than we are covering here and more than we can ever know. Again, we encourage you to commit your life to seeking *the kingdom of God and His righteousness* if you want to know the true and living God. We can never know all there is to know, but we can be a witness of who He reveals Himself to be to each of us.

HOW HE IS HERE

GOD is Spirit (John 4:24), not bound to any place or time, with the prerogative to reveal Himself wherever He pleases.

There is no place we can go from His presence (Psalm 139:3-10).

No one can hide himself from God (Jeremiah 23:23-24).

He sees everything—the evil and the good (Proverbs 15:3).

Though He is omnipresent (in all places at all times) not everyone can witness to this truth. We cannot arrive at the truth of our God from philosophy, science, or any way but through His Word. Natural man cannot come to an understanding of truth, because truth comes from God and is revealed by His Holy Spirit. We can read the Bible, which is God's book, but not understand it except the Spirit of truth interprets for us. Jesus spoke of sending the Holy Spirit for this purpose (John 14:17; John 15:26; John 16:13).

If we read and believe what the Bible says, it will be through the work of the Holy Spirit in us.

We read from the Bible what we believe to be true and live accordingly; this is the faith that His Spirit and His Word work in us. Nothing can shake this faith when we know that God is here with us by His Spirit.

By His Promise
His Word is His promise to reveal Himself and to fulfill every promise that He has made to us as His children.

He promises never to leave us, nor forsake us (Hebrews 13:5).

He is with us; He is our God (Isaiah 41:10).

We understand through faith in His Word by the Holy Spirit that He was incarnate in His Son, Jesus Christ. Let us go now to our next truth.

WHY HE IS HERE
GOD is here ruling and reigning through His Son, Jesus Christ. When Jesus came to earth and lived thirty-three years, it was to fulfill His promise and His purpose to save a people for Himself—a remnant, to share His glory. He lived a perfect life in obedience to the will of His Father, so He could offer Himself as a sacrifice for our sins. That sacrifice offered, His dying to redeem all who believe, resurrected from the dead, ascending back to the

Father, sending the Holy Spirit to rule in each heart, was the plan of redemption. Christ now sits at the right hand of the Father, upholding all things by the word of His power (Hebrews 1:1-3).

"For there is one God, and one mediator between God and men, the man Christ Jesus." 1 Timothy 2:5

Before the foundation of the world He chose His people to be *holy and blameless* before Him. Through the sacrifice of His son, we are led to believe and live as His children (Ephesians 1:3-5).

The promise of the Father to send His Spirit was fulfilled at Pentecost after Christ's ascension (Acts 1:8).

By His Spirit working in us, He is conforming us to the image of His Son, to prepare us for eternity with Him (Romans 3:28-29). In all things that seem unfair and not to our liking, we experience the humbling and meekness of spirit that we need.

We will continue with His promises and purposes in the chapters that follow. It is through these that we will learn more of the truth of Christianity and live beyond our former thoughts and expectations. Writing this and other books is the Lord's means of teaching me what I still need to know. And what a blessing it is to read, study, meditate and memorize His promises, and experience this relationship that He planned for us.

Dear heavenly Father, we understand that your will for us as your children is to know you, Let us continue to know more of who you are as our Creator, Redeemer and Father; to live in anticipation of more than we have experienced, and to be a witness to others of your relationship with us as your redeemed ones, those who are beloved in Christ. Thank you for blessing us with the revelation of who you are by the power of your Holy Spirit. We praise you for bringing us to you through Jesus Christ your Son, whom we love, even as we love you, and in whose name, we praise you and thank you. Amen.

5

I Cannot Write Fast Enough

As I began to write this chapter, my heart overflowed; so much that I did not know what to write first. There was more than enough for another book about the ills of a people in yet another generation that stand and live against the Creator of heaven and earth; a generation that is ignorant of the foundation of civilization, of what makes for freedom and peace. But, that is not why ***my tongue is the pen of a ready writer*** (Psalm 45:1).

It is the overflow Jesus promised from the Holy Spirit to those who come to Him (John 7:37-39), those who are thirsty for something that this world cannot give.

While the world has hung Christianity out to dry—as Christ was hung on a cross—He continues to pour out His blessings from His majestic throne in heaven on those who seek freedom and peace in Him.

The early Monday morning dawns after a day of worship and seeking Him above all things. If the world knew the purpose and benefit of a day set apart for Christ in His glory, they would flock to His church. If they knew the King of kings and Lord of lords, they would put aside the things of this world at least for one day to have the blessings of heaven saturate and consume them.

I cannot, without it flowing into a full-size book, write everything that I continually experience in a relationship that turns me from the chaos of this world and enables me to focus on Christ.

But, just for a bit, let me share His kingdom that is present and powerful in this world, a kingdom I continue to write about, the kingdom that He shares with all His people.

Currently, Jerry and I marvel at how Jesus Christ is real, the same today, as He was when He, with joy, endured the cross for us. Sometimes this is more the miracle than when He rose from the dead. He is present always and speaks in and to every situation.

Snakes in the House
Jerry woke me on a Tuesday night around 4:00, to tell me that there was a snake in the bathroom.

Normally, you would expect the man to take care of these things, but Jerry, being an amputee in a wheelchair, needs me to work things out.

We don't think the snake was poisonous. Nonetheless, in all his (83) and my (80) years and together (58) we had never had to contend with snakes in the house. I say, snakes, because as I was writing this chapter, there was another one under a butterfly net in our other bathroom, discovered the next morning and later, removed by a pest control expert. The first one got away when we were turning on lights and opening the front door; planning to catch him and throw him out.

His Promises
As I lay back down, the words came, "**Fear not, for I am with you. Be not dismayed, for I am your God. I will strengthen you. I will help you. I will uphold you with my righteous, right hand.**" Isaiah 41:10

These words ring true every time.

We never know what will happen next as we live in this wilderness, the wilderness into which God banished our first parents when they refused to listen to Him.

I Can't Write Fast Enough

The world's ills are a combination of the individual ills of all His creatures. Those who follow Christ have to live in the middle of the sin and rebellion of the world.

But we don't have to be slaves to the god of this world, and the news of its continued upheaval. We have a heavenly Father, the God and Father of our Lord Jesus Christ, who lives true to His promises and witnesses through us of His grace and glory.

His Worship

Yesterday's attendance of our Lord to His worship was another experience of His pouring out His blessings for us to carry through this week. To hear again of how He loved us before the foundation of the world; how He proved that love when He sent His Son, and Jesus gave Himself to deliver us from this present evil age; to share this love with our brothers and sisters, is a life that leaves no room for the world's sensationalism.

To write about the kingdom of God and His righteousness is a full-time job; one that I experience more than I can write about. These are worth more than all the world offers.

It is worth all that we have to go through. in this world as we continue toward the promise of eternity with Him.

His Word is the most precious thing to read. To meditate and memorize, to hear it preached, all in the power of His Holy Spirit, is His means of abiding with us and speaking to us in every circumstance.

I could write about all that I experienced yesterday as we jam-packed all that we could in one day, but it would not mean as much to you as it did to me. You had to be there. The personal relationship with the Father and our Lord Jesus Christ is His gift to all His children, those who are born of His Spirit and live by His Spirit.

He must increase—the world and we decrease—in the sight of His grace and glory. In the showers of His blessings, the world is diminished. Satan and his forces are brought to nothing in our eyes and our world. The river of living water showers us with His blessings and washes away the filth of the world (Ephesians 5:26-27).

We see the triumphant Lord of glory ruling above the fading glory of man. He laughs them in derision (Psalm 2).

> **"Why do the heathen rage, and the people imagine a vain thing?**
> **Kiss the Son, lest he be angry, and ye perish from the way, when his wrath is kindled but a little.**
> **Blessed are all they that put their trust in him."**
> **Psalm 2:1, 12**

Gracious Father, as we begin a new week, let us continue to focus upon you through Jesus Christ, your Son, whom you have given to be our Lord. Give us repentant hearts, filled with your Spirit for obedience of faith; that we may live in anticipation of what you have planned for us. Make us to experience the truth of your presence and power. Let your words of grace, truth, love and peace flow and bless others so that they know the reason for our hope and peace. In Jesus' name, I pray. Amen

6

Weakness and Meekness

> "And he said unto me, My grace is sufficient for thee:
> for my strength is made perfect in weakness.
> Most gladly, therefore will I rather glory in my infirmities,
> that the power of Christ may rest upon me."
> 2 Corinthians 12:9

When I began this chapter, there were seven young boys and their soccer coach trapped in a cave in Thailand. They knew that they could not save themselves, to get through the water that had blocked their passageway. Four were brought through the waters by an international team of rescuers, but the others waited. (Eventually all were rescued.)

Could they have shared their thoughts as they waited, no doubt they would admit their weakness in saving themselves and their total dependence on anyone who could save them.

In our natural state, pride causes us to pretend to be strong, rather than admit our weakness. It is in cases of despair that men will admit their weakness, and in meekness, cry out and accept help from anyone who can save them.

> "Therefore I take pleasure in infirmities, in reproaches, in necessities, in persecutions, in distresses for Christ's sake: for when I am weak, then am I strong."
> 2 Corinthians 12:10

The apostle Paul followed in the footsteps of the Master as he endured the hardships of the Christian life. He admitted his weakness, but rather than let his weakness keep him from his work of the gospel, he endured in meekness as he counted that *the power of Christ rested upon him*.

As a disciple of Christ, he suffered in his "infirmities, reproaches, necessities, persecutions, and distress" (2 Corinthians 12:10) for the sake of Christ. If the only result of his suffering was endurance, we might not be impressed, but he understood the reason for his weakness, so he would experience the "strength that is made perfect in weakness." His pleasure was through his suffering as he experienced the strength of Christ in his weakness. When the little "I am" is submitted to Him, the great "I AM" proves His strength.

Beyond a mere Christianity, the conclusion seems to be— weakness plus the power of Christ equals pleasure in the presence and power of Christ, no matter the circumstances.

No wonder Paul lived a life of meekness, in total dependence on the Lord. He understood the Master's words in John 15:4, "Without me you can do nothing."

This *power of Christ* that rested upon Him was the humbling of the Lord in his weakness, enabling him to submit in his weakness to the strength of Christ. Even in prison, he and Silas worshipped; prayed and sang praises unto God (Acts 16:25-34).

> **"I can do all things through Christ,
> which strengtheneth me."**
> Philippians 4:13

Paul understood the role of the creature in relationship to our Creator. He made us weak, so we would need Him. When He left our first parents alone to their free will, He proved they were unable to take care of themselves and to fulfill their purpose.

It is only when we come in our need to the Savior, in weakness, admitting our nothingness and need for Him, that He can save us and be all to us that our Father planned for Him to be.

We must in meekness, in true humility, come to Him and experience the difference He makes in our lives. If we mumble through, thinking we can accomplish anything on our own, we miss the true nature of the Christian life. To be humble is the only means of going beyond a mere Christianity to discover *the power of Christ* and His abundant life within us.

> **"It is the indwelling Christ who will live His life in us, meek and lowly. We must long for this, above everything, seeking this holy secret of the knowledge of the nature of God as He works all. We must set aside our ordinary religion to secure this, the first and chief of the marks of Christ within us. And begin to praise God that there is opened up to you in Jesus a heavenly humility of which you have hardly known, and through which a heavenly blessedness (which you possibly have never yet tasted) can come into you."** Andrew Murray ***Humility, the Beauty of Holiness***2

Dear heavenly Father, how blessed we are that you call us your own, having saved us in Christ, your Son. We praise you that even meekness is the work of your Holy Spirit within us. Enable us to see and admit our weakness and our need for you, so we can glorify you even when we are afflicted and in distress, taking pleasure in your presence and power with us always. In Jesus' name, we pray and praise you. Amen.

(Suggested Reading: <u>A Broad Review of Andrew Murray's Humility</u>

---

2 Waiting on God by Andrew Murray is in public domain

7

Control or Solutions

Treatment for pests has become more intense since we discovered snakes in our bathrooms. The supervisor with the company that covers our termite inspections gave me a lengthy explanation of why their company offers pest solutions instead of the usual pest control. He described the differences in how they would treat one home that might be different in another. Some solutions work for ants and roaches, but not for mice. You certainly would not expect the same treatment for snakes as you would for spiders.

The general rule for rats and snakes is to prevent their entry, which means that you will be charged an enormous free for them to seal all the crevices in your home, including cracks under your roofline. Snakes can climb and get into your attic. They are after the rats that come in the same way.

All this may seem impossible to imagine, especially for old folks like Jerry and me. But it is just more of the same happenings of the wilderness in which we live.

The Glad Rule
Since we started living by the **Glad Rule**, we never cease to find something good in all the episodes we experience. In every event, the Lord teaches us and grows us in our faith in Him (**Romans 8:28-29**; **2 Peter 3:17-18**). We thank the Lord for the snakes. When the exterminator came, he took a video of the water gushing down the back foundation in our basement.

The solution to stop the water was to unclog the downspout. Without the attempts to eradicate the snakes, we would not have known we had a water problem in the basement.

Everything of this physical life seems to have a parallel in the spiritual realm. Andrew Murray stated in his book *Waiting on God* that "all nature becomes a preacher" in our relationship with God.

In this case, my thoughts for this chapter ran to a recent sermon on the first commandment from the book of Exodus. The difference in the physical and the spiritual—God gave the commandments for His people to reveal their sin and His requirements. Though they are the rules of His kingdom, He knew they would not control the sins in our lives. That was like putting a No Trespassing sign outside our home for the pests. Even if they could read, they would not understand. They would still come into any opening available. God posted what He wanted, but the commandments were, as Paul wrote in **Galatians 3,** only a precursor to what He would accomplish through the life, death, and resurrection of His Son. The law could not keep His people from their habit of disobedience.

The solution for treatment needed in our lives would come later.

> "Wherefore the law was our schoolmaster to bring us unto Christ, that we might be justified by faith." Galatians 3:24

The difference in how the Lord works as our exterminator is, that He covers His people with the blood of Christ. He draws us to the cross where we are washed in the blood of the Lamb. He covers the crevices. No place is left open to the enemy of our souls.

We are filled with His Holy Spirit, saturated with the counsel of God and under a consuming fire, being **kept by His power until the day of Christ's return** (**1 Peter 1:5**).

Control or Solutions

His Word continues to fill us with His grace, written on our hearts and in our minds, spoken by His Spirit within us to remind us of who He is and whose we are. We are His dwelling place, and will He not take care of His house? Let us relinquish all to Him—for His glory and our joy.

> "And they overcame him by the blood of the Lamb, and by the word of their testimony; and they loved not their lives unto the death." Revelation 12:11

Gracious Father, we have no defense of our own; no solution for the cleansing of our sin, except by your provision for us. Fill us with the power of your Holy Spirit, the Spirit of our Lord and Savior Jesus Christ, in whose name we pray and live. Amen .

8

The New Nature of the True Christian

The heart, spirit, and life of a Christian are different than an ordinary person's life. There is an extraordinary, supernatural working of God's grace that reforms and transforms the center of all things. It is inbred and expressed outwardly by the Holy Spirit of God. It is the life of Christ that is manifest within and without, permeating the whole being and perpetuating forever a new creation through which He reveals His grace and His glory.

Here we suggest three main factors of a true Christian life that radiate from Christ within us. Love, humility, and holiness are the evidence of the new heart and spirit that were promised in Ezekiel 36:26 - God's working of new life in a fallen world.

All that God promised since the fall is being fulfilled by the Spirit of Christ through His people, restoring His image through the life and work of Christ for our salvation and His glory. Knowledge and truth are included in this triangle, as Christ, Himself, is "the way, the truth, and the life." (John 14:6) It is in His Word, the written word, The Holy Bible, and the living word, Jesus Christ, that we know God and His purpose for our creation and redemption. It is His means of revealing Himself and the work of grace within us. In our continual reading, study, meditation, and memorization, we understand what He is doing; throughout our lives revealing and fulfilling His plans for us, in us, and through us.

LOVE ~ the love of God, the Father, is evidence from His own heart and nature given to each of His children. This love, unlike any of our imaginations of love, is the new nature. It is the root and the fruit of all that God is and does; and works in all to whom He has given the heart and spirit of Christ. Love works in every area of the new life. Through His revelation of our justification, forgiveness, and restoration in Christ, we see the evidence of His love (1 John 4:10), and the working of this love through us for Him and others (1 John 3:16).

HUMILITY ~ the humility of the Father and the Son, Jesus Christ, who gave Himself to suffer and sacrifice His life for us that we might bear His image, His nature, and disposition. Obedience of faith, patience, kindness, and faithfulness are the results of Christ's humility in and through us. We see His humility and ours in Philippians 2:3-8.

The New Nature of a True Christian

HOLINESS ~ the outward working of Christ and the Holy Spirit in the life of the Christian; a return to God of what He has given; the evidence to the angels in heaven and the world of the difference in the life of a Christian. This is a purity and goodness that only God can work in human life.

> "See what kind of love the Father has given to us, that we should be called children of God; and so, we are. The reason why the world does not know us is that it did not know him. Beloved, we are God's children now, and what we will be has not yet appeared; but we know that when he appears we shall be like him, because we shall see him as he is. And everyone who thus hopes in him purifies himself as he is pure."
> 1 John 3:1-3

Dear Father in heaven, what mercy you have shown us, and that you continue to work in us. Fill us anew today with your Spirit; with the life of Christ, to know and do your will. Through us reveal to others the magnitude of your grace—for your glory and our joy. In Jesus' name I pray. Amen.

9

Endear and Endure

**"Hereby perceive we the love of God,
because he laid down his life for us:
and we ought to lay down our lives for the brethren."**
1 John 3:16

If the Lord brings us to the heights of Christianity—*Beyond a Mere Christianity*—it will be according to the truth that the apostle writes here. What keeps us from reaching this height? It must be that we do not *perceive the love of God*, who, in Christ *laid down his life for us*. To *perceive* is to see with a spiritual reality—beyond our physical sight—how much He loves us and how He proved His love. We will look in depth in two other chapters at how His great love works in the hearts of His children but for this one, we are led to write of those who, with time and experience of His grace, know the presence and power of the Holy Spirit of Christ working His own nature and disposition through them in relationship with others.

Several years ago, even with the *new birth* (John 3:3), there was no real understanding of the difference He would make in my life. Baptism at the age of eleven did not change my heart; self-centeredness was still my nature. Years later, God's Holy Spirit speaking through His Holy Word gave me a *new heart and spirit* (Ezekiel 36:26). It was then I longed for the life of Christ within me.

Repentance and faith was a work of His goodness and mercy in me (Romans 2:4); the effect of His Spirit in the *new heart and spirit* within me.

Everything changed on that beautiful day in 1992 when He brought me to Himself. And I never looked back.

His Endearment
He endeared Himself to me, speaking through the written Word and His Spirit so I could see Him as the loving Creator and Redeemer that He is. Since then, He has been an ever-present guide and protector of my mind, heart, and spirit. He has endured with me through all the trials and adversities Jerry and I have encountered. The more affliction we experience, the more of His love and care His Holy Spirit ministers to us and the more we can see and care for others. We continue to *grow in grace and the knowledge of our Lord Jesus Christ* (2 Peter 3:18). We could speak of many trials we have endured, but time and space do not permit here. We have published eleven other books that witness of His presence and teachings.

Most and best of all is how He endears Himself through us to others. We wrote of this experience in *One Month to Live ~ A Father's Last Words*, the story of God's abundant grace as I cared for my dad during the last three weeks of his life.

Never would I have known that being a caregiver for my dad, for grandchildren, for my mother with dementia and for Jerry the last thirteen years, would have prepared me to practice this endearment. We, together, have learned to see the needs of others; to pray for them; to reach out to any that the Lord shows us. We don't have to look far. Within our own family and our church family, there are many who need encouragement. Just a word of support and hope is enough for most. These are the closest to us and the ones with which we have developed lasting relationships. *In Prayer and In Touch* is our email prayer ministry, whereby we stay in touch as we pray for others.

Seeing the Needs of Others
We are enabled to see the needs of others when we go for Jerry's appointments. We may never see some of these again, but the Lord knows what they need. A smile, a "thank you," a word of greeting or a short conversation can leave a lasting impression to the glory of our Lord.

It is those who are the closest, whose needs we know and with whom we endure through their difficulties, sharing the promises of God's Word, praying for special needs, taking a meal, etc. Whatever is needful, the Lord provides through us, His people.

We encourage those who are continually experiencing the hardships of this life to see others in need and pray with the desire to know how to help them. Focus on the Lord and His will in how we can care for others greatly changes how we see our own needs. It is good for the soul to count others in greater need than ourselves.

Is this what John meant in 1 John 3:16? What does it mean to lay down our lives? I believe it means that we first give ourselves to the Lord as the ap**ostle Paul speaks in** 2 Corinthians 8:5. I have had TWO FULL PLATES in caring for Jerry for the last thirteen years but this does not keep me from seeing the needs of others, praying and reaching out when the Lord leads. He always provides more room on our plates for others and gives the extra strength that we need and extra servings of joy when we help and encourage others. We are, by His mercy to us, called to offer our bodies as *living sacrifices* to serve Him and others (Romans 12:1-2).

He Endured for His People
He endured the wrath and punishment for our sins, so we as His people could be united in our love for Him and one another; to bear one another's burdens (Galatians 6:1-2).

Jesus, now and forever, endears Himself to us and endures with us as our Lord and High Priest. It is when we endear ourselves to each other and endure with one another that we are stronger.

As we are united in Christ, members of one body, we stand against the enemy with great power. His Spirit is revealed through those who "in lowliness of mind esteem others better than themselves; who look not on his own things, but on the things of others." Philippians 2:3-4

Father in heaven, open our eyes and hearts. Draw us heavenward to receive your humility, grace and love that extends to others—for your glory and our joy. In Jesus' name, I pray. Amen

10

Three Powerful Words

If we are to get beyond a mere Christianity, we must know the language. In 2016, an article titled *Three Obstacles to Spiritual Growth* listed *Words* as the main obstacle, followed by *Feelings* and *Influences*. I did not realize until I reviewed that article, they are three words we write about here.

Not many Christians are familiar with or use these three words; yet they are significant in what we believe and how we live. Are these words used in normal conversation? No, but it is necessary for a Christian to know and understand them. We cannot just say, "I love Jesus." These powerful words give true meaning to why and how we love Him.

Propitiation, justification and *sanctification* originate with the Father, the Son and The Holy Spirit. Since these are not man's words but God's Words, we need to review them often and meditate on them with the Biblical references. I write this chapter with the same need as others *through every generation to understand:* All three words end in the suffix "ation" meaning "action or process."

1. *what God planned for His people,*
2. *how he established His plan through His Son*
3. *how He executes His plan by the power of His Holy Spirit*

PROPITIATION G2434

Propitiation in Greek is *hilasmós*, properly, *propitiation*; an offering to *appease (satisfy)* an *angry, offended* party.

It is used in 1 John 4 and in Romans 5, both times of *Christ's atoning* blood that *appeases God's wrath, on all confessed sin.* By the *sacrifice* of *Himself*, Jesus Christ provided the ultimate *hilasmós* ("propitiation"). biblehub.com

Before the foundation of the world, in planning a kingdom and a family for Himself, God our heavenly Father made a covenant of redemption with His Son, Jesus Christ (2 Timothy 1:9). This covenant would provide the work and conditions of His grace, whereby He would reveal His love for His people, and by His Holy Spirit, draw them to Himself. Just as His work of Creation, the *action and the process* of Redemption would be His and His alone.

Why and how does a Christian love Jesus?

> "Herein is love, not that we loved God, but that he loved us, and sent his Son to be the propitiation for our sins."
> 1 John 4:10

God shows us His love in all generations through the sacrifice of His Son for us over 2000 years ago. He planned to give up His own Son to as a means to appease His wrath against us. (Who can understand this love?) He gave His Son to give us life, so we would live eternally with Him. Someone's blood has to appease His anger against sin. It will be His or ours. Someone has to pay—we or His Son. He was the perfect "Lamb that was slain." Only God could provide such a sacrifice for us.

I remember the word "propitiation" by syllables. The prefix "pro" indicates a professional able to perform. The center of the word is "pit" where Jesus finds us. "I" am between the "pit" and "ation" whereby His is the action bringing me out of the "pit." O, what love that gives all He is and has. He could give all for us

Three Powerful Words

through His death; through His resurrection and ascension He would gain His own life again and give life to all who are drawn to Him in faith and repentance.

PROPITIATION and JUSTIFICATION

We learn in God's Word the connection between PROPITIATION and JUSTIFICATION—through the righteousness of Jesus.

Romans 3:24-26 incorporates "propitiation" and "justification" through the sinless life of Jesus Christ that qualifies Him for propitiation that leads to our justification.

> "Being *justified* freely by his grace through the redemption that is in Christ Jesus:
> Whom God hath set forth to be a *propitiation* through faith in his blood, to declare his righteousness for the remission of sins that are past, through the forbearance of God;
> To declare, I say, at this time his righteousness: that he might be *just*, and the *justifier* of him which believeth in Jesus."

JUSTIFICATION G1347

dikaíōsis (dik-ah'-yo-sis) from G1344 acquittal (for Christ's sake

The act of God declaring men free from guilt and acceptable to him.

Whereas God planned for the blood of Christ to appease His anger for our sins, He planned through Christ to justify His own actions in pronouncing us "Not guilty" for our sins. It is a forensic term as if applied in a court of law.

Notice in the following references the terms "offences" "judgment" and "condemnation."

> "Who was delivered for our offences and was raised again for our *justification*." Romans 4:25

> "And not as it was by one that sinned, so is the gift: for the judgment was by one to condemnation, but the free gift is of many offences unto justification." Romans 5:16

> *Justification* is the judicial act of God, by which he pardons all the sins of those who believe in Christ. It proceeds on the imputing or crediting to the believer by God himself of the perfect righteousness, active and passive, of his Representative and Surety, Jesus Christ (Romans 10:3-9). *Justification* is not the forgiveness of a man without righteousness, but a declaration that he possesses a righteousness which perfectly and for ever satisfies the law, namely, Christ's righteousness 2 Corinthians 5:21; (Romans 4:6-8). Bible Study Tools

We have advanced in our understanding of the connection between PROPITATION and JUSTIFICATION. Now, let us see the connection between JUSTIFICATION and SANCTIFICATION–the work and power of the Holy Spirit in the life of the believer.

> "The act of faith which thus secures our justification also at the same time secures our *sanctification* (q.v.); and thus the doctrine of *justification* by faith does not lead to licentiousness (**Romans 6:2-7**). Good works, while not the ground, are the certain consequence of justification (6:14; 7:6)."
> *Bible Study Tools*

SANTIFICATION
The word sanctification is not found in the Old Testament, but we make references to the things God sanctified, things that were set apart, consecrated as holy for Him; the seventh day, places of worship, priests.

Three Powerful Words

New Testament G37
hagiozo, to make holy, consecrate, to regard as special (sacred) sanctify.

The word carries somewhat of a different meaning in the New Testament as it refers to a personal ongoing action or process on God's part for His people.

While *propitiation* and *justification* are one-time actions and already accomplished for all His people, *sanctification* is an ongoing action and process in making us holy; enabling us to live a consecrated life to Him as He is preparing us for eternity with Him.

As stated earlier: To show His love for us, God, the Father, planned, and in His timing sent His Son to be a *propitiation* for our sins. Jesus fulfilled the covenant of redemption (the covenant of grace) living a perfect life in obedience to the will of the Father. He was offered as a sacrifice for us, appeasing God's wrath against us; was buried, and resurrected, securing our *justification*. That being finished, He ascended to the right hand of the Father as our High Priest to intercede for us. He sent the Holy Spirit to continue His work of *sanctification* in each generation until Christ comes again.

Let's follow the process from Christ's work on the cross to the supernatural work of the Holy Spirit in our hearts and lives.

> "Christ also loved the church, and gave himself for it; That he might *sanctify and cleanse it with the washing of water by the word*, That he might present it to himself a glorious church, not having spot, or wrinkle, or any such thing; but that it should be holy and without blemish." Ephesians 5:25-27

> "But of him are ye in Christ Jesus, who of God is made unto us wisdom, and righteousness, and sanctification, and redemption." 1 Corinthians 1:30

Paul explains *sanctification* of the Spirit in 2 Thessalonians 2:13.

> "God hath from the beginning chosen you to salvation through sanctification of the Spirit and belief of the truth:"

Simon Peter uses the same terms in 1 Peter 1:2,

> "Elect according to the foreknowledge of God the Father, through sanctification of the Spirit, unto obedience and sprinkling of the blood of Jesus Christ:

Propitiation leads to *justification*, and justification through the power of His Spirit in our *sanctification* brings us in obedience to Christ, the perfect plan of salvation *before the foundation of the world* (Ephesians 1:3; 2 Timothy 1:9).

Gracious and holy Father in heaven, how can we understand such a holy love and the power of your love, except as you send your Holy Spirit to do this great and mighty work in us. We praise you for your plans and ask that you continue working in our hearts and lives all that you desire for us—all to your glory and our joy. In Jesus' name we thank you and praise you. Amen.

11

The Right Man for the Job

Last year we were blessed to find an air-conditioning contractor who knew how our 21-year-old unit works. When we built our house in this small neighborhood, Jackson EMC was doing a joint project for the geo-thermal system and paid all but $3000. Expecting more than we knew was possible for a unit with an average life of 18 years, we tried one more contractor after the last one did all he could. Joe, from North Hall Heating and Air, answered our online request for someone who knows this system.

He charged $45 for a service call, with a guarantee to repair. He came a second time with an expert he had known for over twenty years, a friend who retired after working with geo-thermal systems in huge projects. He sat down with Jerry and me to explain how the system works and why we should think of replacing the unit. While he was talking, Joe was working in the basement. We gently stopped his presentation (thinking of what this was costing us) and asked him to get to the chase. What was his advice at this point? Even if there was a short-term solution, we would eventually need a new unit.

The expert left; Joe came upstairs, saying he had changed two connections. He left with no assurance of what he had done, but with no extra charge. We asked for an estimate for a new unit, expecting the inevitable. We know that in the next year or two, we may be down-sizing again, and we will have to replace the system before we sell our home.

But, since Joe was here the last time, we have had *heat* for the winter and *cool* air for the summer. This past month's bill was $118.00, almost unheard of, even for a 2000 sq. ft. all-electric house.

In the middle of our adversities, this and other physical blessings help us know the Lord's continual care for us. We still need other contractors, including a technician to rid our house of ants and roaches (the one we were using failed after trying for two years).

Where is all this leading? Where does this chapter fit to bring us beyond a mere Christianity?

Our Spiritual House
How far do we go to find the man that has the knowledge and equipment to control the temperature in our physical house? We continue to search until we find the right man for the job.

Who has the expertise to fix what is needed in our spiritual house—the outdated workings of the human soul?

There is only one "right" man who knows the heart and the soul; who is qualified to come into the basement of our lives, to examine, evaluate, and estimate the cost of replacement.

The system that provides the air conditioning for our lives is an eternal system, and the continual connection with Christ and His Spirit to the Father above.

> "but you have received the Spirit of adoption as sons, by whom we cry, 'Abba! Father!'
> The Spirit himself bears witness with our spirit that we are children of God," (Romans 8:14-17)

The Cost
This continual comfort comes by His own cost: a holy life in humility and submission to the whole law of God, His "righteousness" as ours, His life given as a sacrifice, His blood shed for the final price. Our final cost—our whole life given for

His. This is the life of a true Christian. This is no mere Christianity. Jesus Christ our Lord and Savior went beyond anything we could have imagined, even what had been prophesied, to bring us beyond what we could ask or think of life.

What should we ask ourselves? Is our desire for comfort in this world based on our physical needs, or do we long for something more, based on what God is able and promises to do?

Call to Me
We make the calls for our physical needs. He bids us to call Him for all of life.

> "Call to me and I will answer you, and will tell you great and hidden things that you have not known." Jeremiah 33:3

> "Delight yourself in the Lord and He will give you the desires of your heart." Psalm 37:4

We delight ourselves in the Lord when we come to the end of ourselves. And when we find our delight in Him, we desire to desire what He desires, even to the point of suffering for Him.

His eternal comfort and delight are ours when He makes the right connection for us.

There is only one "right" man. No other religion promises what Jehovah, the Lord our God promises. No other has the power to do what the Lord does, for, in, and through His people

> **"For there is one God,
> and one mediator between God and men,
> the man Jesus Christ."**
> 1 Timothy 2:15

Our Father in heaven, Father of lights, Father of glory, having sent your Son, the Lord of glory, we praise you; for your Holy Spirit we thank you---for your wisdom and knowledge hidden in Christ and revealed to us in your Word and by the power of your Holy Spirit which we could never afford. We praise you that you planned before Creation to provide all that we would need here and for eternity through your Son, our Lord and Savior—all for your glory and our joy. In His precious and powerful name, we pray. Amen.

12

A Holy, High, and Heavenly Calling

If we are to live beyond a mere Christianity, we must understand that Christianity is not man's idea, it is a calling from God. From the highest heaven, God created all things for His own purpose; in His plans He brings us into a relationship with Him through His Son Jesus Christ. He rules and reigns through His Son, and by His Holy Spirit calls us to follow Him, to know Him and to live for Him.

A Holy Calling

> "Who hath saved us, and called us with an holy calling, not according to our works, but according to his own purpose and grace, which was given us in *Christ Jesus* before the world began," 2 Timothy 1:9

It is a holy calling from a Holy God, who calls us to a separation from the world to live holy before Him (1 Peter 1:15) and to serve Him in His kingdom. We cannot work for this relationship but He, by His own purpose, reveals His grace to us in Christ. This was determined *before the world began*, made possible through His Son, and administered by His Holy Spirit.

A High Calling

> "I press toward the mark for the prize of the *high calling* of God in *Christ Jesus*." Philippians 3:14

The Apostle Paul knew the calling of a Christian to be the *high calling* of God in Christ, where Christ sits enthroned at the right hand of the Father, ruling and reigning as King of kings and Lord of lords. This *high calling* is beyond our earthly thinking and comes from above.

A Heavenly Calling

> "Wherefore, *holy* brethren, partakers of the *heavenly calling*, consider the Apostle and High Priest of our profession, *Christ Jesus*." Hebrews 3:1

The writer of Hebrews 2 spoke of Jesus being made like us, *partakers of flesh and blood, made a High Priest for us, being tempted Himself, so that He can succor those who are tempted* (Hebrews 2:17-18).

The Purpose

What is the purpose of His *calling*, and what are the expected results? We find this explained vividly in Paul's letter to the church at Thessalonica. To get the full impact of this calling and the result, we should read 2 Thessalonians 1. Paul writes, describing their *patience and grace* through the endurance of *persecution and tribulation*.

This calling includes the testing of our faith by those *who do not obey the gospel*.

"that ye may be counted worthy of the kingdom of God, for which ye also suffer" (2 Thessalonians 1:5).

"Wherefore also we pray always for you, that our God would count you worthy of this *calling*, and fulfil all the good pleasure of his goodness, and the work of faith with power:" 2 Thessalonians 1:11

This holy, high and heavenly calling begins and ends with our Lord God in heaven; with His intentions to create and redeem a people with all the good pleasure of *His goodness*.

"That the name of our Lord Jesus Christ may be glorified in you, and ye in him, according to the grace of our God and the Lord Jesus Christ." 2 Thessalonians 1:12

Paul speaks of the reasons we are called:
Called *to be saints* (1 Corinthians 1:2) *into the fellowship of His Son, Jesus Christ* (1 Corinthians 1:9); *into His kingdom and glory* (*1 Thessalonians 2:12*):

Simon Peter makes reference in the following:
Called out of darkness into His marvelous light (1 Peter 2:9); *that we should inherit a blessing* (1 Peter 3:9); *called to His eternal glory in Christ* (1 Peter 5:10); *to glory and virtue* (2 Peter 1:3).

The Work of Grace
Look at the *Holy Calling* in 2 Timothy 1:9 in the previous text—"according to His own *purpose* and *grace* which was given us in Christ Jesus before the world began." In every generation He is *calling* His saints, and by His grace, *working faith in us with power* not only to believe but to suffer for the sake of His name and the gospel.

The common denominator, *Christ Jesus*, is found in every reference to God's *holy, high and heavenly calling.*

Gracious Father, who has called us, according to your purpose and the precious grace that works in the hearts of those whom you call, we thank you. We praise you for saving us and calling us to a life beyond any mere thoughts of faith that man can speak of; a faith that enables us to suffer for your sake and to endure to the end. Your Son, our Lord, Savior and High Priest calls us to follow in His footsteps. Do your work in our hearts to see beyond this world to the place of our calling and glorify your Son in us. In His precious name I pray. Amen.

13

Covenant Living and Giving

Life beyond a mere Christianity is possible in covenant with God the Father and His Son Jesus Christ. God relates to His creatures only through covenant.

> "All true theology is based on some form of a divine covenant. The Christian religion must be understood covenantally, for that is how God has chosen to relate to man, whether in the garden or after the entrance of sin into the world. The goal of all divine–human covenants is summed up in the words found throughout the Bible: "I will be your God and you will be my people, and I will dwell among you" (Exodus 6:7; 29:45; Ezekiel 11:20; 2 Corinthians 6:16; Revelation 21:3) *What is a Covenant?*

A covenant is an agreement between two or more parties. There is an initiator, one who is responsible to reveal the covenant to another person. We can do all we can, thinking we live in relationship to God, with little success, until we understand how God initiates His covenant with His people.

With the initiation, He provides the conditions and the means to live in covenant with Him. Just as He created us without our help, He has chosen us as His people. He presents His covenant to us with the promise to fulfill every detail and draws us to Christ by His Holy Spirit.

We enter His covenant with Him by faith, believing that He has the power to complete all He specifies in the covenant.

The Covenant of Grace
His is a covenant of grace—the only covenant of grace—which requires no work of our own; a covenant of redemption through Jesus Christ, who has fulfilled the conditions; a covenant of love between Him and His people.

This short chapter cannot do justice to the subject of the covenants presented to Adam (a covenant of works), everlasting covenants to Noah (Genesis 9:16), Abraham (Genesis 17:7) Isaac (Genesis 17:19) and David (2 Samuel 23:5), and fulfilled by the life and blood of our Lord Jesus Christ (Hebrews 13:20-21). His Holy Spirit continues to complete the Father's covenant in us for the promised inheritance that is ours through His Son, our Lord and Savior.

The Lord of the Covenant
Covenant living and giving is possible when we know the person who has the power to fulfill all the conditions for both sides. Much can be said about life in covenant with our heavenly Father through His Son and the power of His Holy Spirit.

I cannot in my own words express how the father of our faith, Abraham, lived in covenant with our heavenly Father, but if you have ever wondered how and why God could ask Abraham to sacrifice his only son, please take the time for the following message. I pray that, as I was, you may be encouraged to live and give as our Father and our Lord did for us. Don't miss a blessing—please check the link below.

Abraham's Fiery Trial
https://www.sermonaudio.com/sermoninfo.asp?SID=72918121106

Dear Father, I pray that you would speak to other hearts through this sermon, even as you did to mine. Teach us what it means to live in covenant with you, to give all to you, for your glory and our joy. In Jesus' name, I pray, Amen

14

Seeing IS Believing

God gave us eyes to see the beauty of His creation. It is easy for us to see physically and to be distracted by the things of this world; to settle for the status quo. To see beyond a mere Christianity requires three things: *light, revelation,* and *new eyes.* And these three come from God through His Son, Jesus Christ by the power of His Holy Spirit.

At the foundation of the world God said, "Let there be light." Before there was a sun or moon, there was light, simply by His Word. Jesus was identified as the Light and the Word from heaven. He opened heaven for us to reveal the Father/Creator and heaven itself in Him.

All this—beyond this world—is revealed in God's Word, the Holy Bible. There was darkness before God said, "Let there be light." We cannot see in the dark. So, it is with human hearts.

When speaking to Nicodemus, who came to him *at night*, Jesus knew His real need, "and said unto him, Verily, verily, I say unto thee, 'Except a man be born again, he cannot see the kingdom of God.'" John 3:3

This is reflected in Ezekiel 36:26 regarding the promise that the Lord would give His people *a new heart and a new spirit*, taking away *the heart of stone* and rebellion against Him. With *the new heart and spirit* come eyes of faith to see what others cannot see; to understand the things of God.

Jesus said to His disciples:

> "For verily I say unto you, that many prophets and righteous men have desired to see those things which ye see, and have not seen them; and to hear those things which ye hear, and have not heard them." Matthew 13:17

To the religious leaders and others who heard him:

> "But I said unto you, That ye also have seen me, and believe not." John 6:36

> "Your father Abraham rejoiced to see my day: and he saw it, and was glad." John 8:56

> "And Jesus said, For judgment I am come into this world, that they which see not might see; and that they which see might be made blind." John 9:39

> "And he that seeth me seeth him that sent me." John 12:4

> "And this is the will of him that sent me, that every one which seeth the Son, and believeth on him, may have everlasting life: and I will raise him up at the last day." John 6:40

> "Blessed are the pure in heart: for they shall see God." Matthew 5:8

The eyes of faith enable us to see and endure through the most difficult trials. Stephen spoke of heaven opened to him in his persecution.

"But he, being full of the Holy Ghost, looked up stedfastly into heaven, and saw the glory of God, and Jesus standing on the right hand of God, And said, Behold, I see the heavens opened, and the Son of man standing on the right hand of God." Acts 7:55-56

Seeing IS Believing

"As one looks and discovers that almost everything down here is in confusion, chaos, and ruins, it seems as though Satan were getting the better of the conflict. But as one looks above, instead of around, there is plainly visible to the eye of faith a Throne, a Throne unaffected by the storms of earth, a Throne that is set, stable and secure; and upon it is seated One whose name is the Almighty, and who "worketh all things after the counsel of His own will" (Ephesians 1:11). This then is our confidence—God *is on the Throne*. Though God's governing hand is invisible to the eye of sense, it is real to faith, that faith which rests with sure confidence upon His Word, and therefore is assured *He cannot fail*." A. W. Pink *The Sovereignty of God* [3]

We find in Hebrews 11 a list of those who saw Jesus and heaven with eyes of faith; who endured to the end. And as spoken of Moses:

"By faith he forsook Egypt, not fearing the wrath of the king: for he endured, as seeing him who is invisible." Hebrews 11:27

And these are the promises that the world cannot see.

"Even the Spirit of truth; whom the world cannot receive, because it seeth him not, neither knoweth him: but ye know him; for he dwelleth with you, and shall be in you." John 14:17

"But as it is written, To whom he was not spoken of, they shall see: and they that have not heard shall understand." Romans 15:21

---

[3] *The Sovereignty of God* by A.W. Pink in public domain

Paul prayed for "the eyes of understanding to be enlightened." (Ephesians 1:18).

> "To open their eyes, and to turn them from darkness to light, and from the power of Satan unto God, that they may receive forgiveness of sins, and inheritance among them which are sanctified by faith that is in me." Acts 26:18

How we see determines our joy in this life.
To see Christ is to live joyfully in anticipation of eternity with Him, "even in this vale of sin, for he illumines and gives the beauty of grace, forgiveness, and hope. When the curtain of this life drops, it will rise to the sight of his loving gaze, his exalted splendor, his unending, satisfying presence." Chris Strevel

> "Whom having not seen, ye love; in whom, though now ye see him not, yet believing, ye rejoice with joy unspeakable and full of glory:" 1 Peter 1:8

> "and we shall be like him, for we shall see Him as He is." (1 John 3:2).

Gracious Father in heaven, thank you for sending the Great Physician to be your light in our darkness; for birthing us into your kingdom with a new heart, spirit, eyes, and life in Him. Fill us with your Spirit of truth—the Spirit of Christ—that we may see you and live in light of your glory. This is our joy. In Jesus' name, I pray. Amen

15

How Exciting is Your God?

For this chapter, I had thought to use a snippet from a dormant file. Writing this book has only served to stir up the Spirit within me to the truths in an unfinished book. *Worship That Springs from the Heart of God ~ A Sheep's View* was an exciting work several years ago that became more than I could finish. (Other books in the series Little Books About the Magnitude of God are no more than 100 pages.) A Table of Contents for two sections, The Meaning of Worship and The Means of Worship including chapters of Roles and Positions, Rules and Conditions, brought me to that Spring that flows from the heart of God. Worship became something new and powerful in my heart and life.

I learned and now experience the connection—the vital connection between God's Word and His Worship; with a capital W; beyond a mere worship. In studying what it means to worship and praise the Lord, I related it to my grandchildren (an older sheep teaching younger sheep) by asking, "How exciting is your God?"

This depends on how He "incites" us.

INCITE
He first "provokes the action" by His Word and Spirit through my mind and heart—instruments He created for this purpose.

The word "provoke" is used many times in the Old and New Testaments to speak of provoking God and others to anger and jealousy.

There is only one reference that speaks of the power to *provoke unto love and good works*.

> "And let us consider one another to provoke unto love and to good works:" Hebrews 10:24

Paroxysmo (pä-ro-ksü-smo's) first means *incite, incitement* or second, *irritate, contention*.
(Had I not reviewed this for this chapter, I would not have found this little nugget hidden in plain view.)

It is the Spirit of God, the Spirit of Christ, who speaks through His written word, revealing the God who is worthy to be worshiped. The Living Word, Jesus Christ, lives within us to bring the worthy worship that He desires and deserves.

EXCITE
As I read and hear His word of truth, He does a work within me that "excites" me.

Through His Word from His own heart, by His Spirit, He quickens my spirit (Romans 8:11). This understanding brings more light to Paul's writing in 1 Corinthians 2, which is worthy for meditation in this matter of how the Spirit works to give us *the mind of Christ*.

> "And my speech and my preaching was not with enticing words of man's wisdom, but in demonstration of the Spirit and of power:
> That your faith should not stand in the wisdom of men, but in the power of God." 2 Corinthians 2:4-5

RECITE
Worship is the continual effect of God's own work within us.
Worship is the "reciting" of His Word and how He teaches us to relate to Him, the result of the Spirit of Christ working from within. No man can do this for me. No man can teach me how to worship the Almighty God, my heavenly Father.

Worship begins with the new birth. With *a new heart and a new spirit* come an understanding of the object of worship. This new creation lives by faith in a God I cannot see.

> "But without faith it is impossible to please him: for he that cometh to God must believe that he is, and that he is a rewarder of them that diligently seek him." Hebrews 11:6

Worship is the reward of our diligence in seeking him. To seek Him through prayer and His written Word is a daily act of worship.

From His Heart to Ours
From His heart "inciting" our hearts for daily worship, He leads us in family worship and then to corporate worship on the Lord's Day with His people "in the assembly of saints." All of this, from the individual to the family, to the church, is the preparation for that glorious gathering as one people in Christ, for an eternal worship (Ephesians 1:10).

> "Wherefore, my beloved, as ye have always obeyed, not as in my presence only, but now much more in my absence, work out your own salvation with fear and trembling. For it is God which worketh in you both to will and to do of his good pleasure." Philippians 2:12-13

HE INITIATES, CALLS, and SAVES with His whole heart and soul.

"Yea, I will rejoice over them to do them good, and I will plant them in this land assuredly with my whole heart and with my whole soul." Jeremiah 32:41

Worship is more than a mere gathering on any one day of the week; it is a continual practice of the Christian life.

"And to love him with all the heart, and with all the understanding, and with all the soul, and with all the strength, and to love his neighbour as himself, is more than all whole burnt offerings and sacrifices." Mark 12:33

A Gripping, Thrilling and Fulfilling Life

The truth of the gospel of the Lord Jesus Christ produces a gripping and thrilling Life in Christ. The law of God that commands our worship comes alive in Christ—incited in us. To love His law is to love Him and worship accordingly (Psalm 1:2-3). Even in the middle of adversity, we can praise Him and worship through His Spirit and the power of His word that speaks to our difficulties. His Spirit is in us and surrounding us (Acts 17:28). He fills us with His grace, nestles us in His goodness, and wraps us in His glory.

The same worship He deserved at the beginning of time is the same worship He incites in us today. HE HAS NOT CHANGED, but He changes us, humbles us, then exalts us to praise Him in an acceptable worship.

Glorious, holy Father, we thank you that worship is not man-induced. We need no enticing words or actions from men to worship you. You are excitement enough. You have made Jesus Christ our worship leader, a worship that is your work in our hearts and lives—the new life in Christ. By Him, let us offer up to you the sacrifice of praise continually, that is, the fruit of our lips giving thanks unto your name. In Jesus' name we pray. Amen.

16

Good Works

Study for this chapter (as many others) has been in process for years as I have gleaned references to "good works" from a continual study in God's Word. It has been a blessing for me to put together these truths and to share them.

Especially, I write this for three types of people: 1. *those who think they have to work for their salvation*; 2. *those whose salvation has made them fruitful, but who overextend themselves thinking they can never do enough*; 3. *those who are fruitful in "good works" because they live in full dependence in the Lord's working in and through them.*

1. Many people fit into the first category, taught that they must put in a certain number of hours of service in their lifetime, to merit God's approval. They believe they have to measure up to the guidelines set by their religious leaders. Their good works supposedly produce a good life and entrance into heaven.

I am reminded of the words sung by Julie Andrews playing the role of Maria von Trapp in *Sound of Music*. In the garden scene, in response to Georg von Trapp's proposal, she sings, "Somewhere in my youth or childhood, I must have done something good."

2. We count in the second category those of the Christian faith who enjoy their service to the Lord and His church. "Good works" for some of these include sacrificing family relationships to serve God. They cannot do enough to satisfy their own expectations.

Years ago, as a young mother, I committed myself to the church in many roles. Jerry traveled in his job, leaving me with time other women didn't have; sometimes giving 200% without realizing that I was taking time away from my children. I remember growing up in the church with the main emphasis on the Great Commission and evangelism. Being a missionary became the ideal for many young women. One of today's para-church organization's main thrust is to send young women to the mission field.

We have known such young women to give up thoughts of marriage hoping their work for Christ is pleasing to Him. Their lives have ended in disappointment, burning out after years of traveling and serving in foreign countries, with no hope for the future.

> 3. In the third category are those who have learned through service and experience that the only "good works" acceptable to God are those that He works through them. These rely on the presence and the power of His Holy Spirit to teach, lead and fill them with wisdom, strength and grace.

In the following references, we will see what the Lord teaches about "good works."

Jeremiah 48:7 speaks of the result of trusting in our own works. Jesus spoke of those who *prophesied in His name, cast out devils and in His name had done many wonderful* **works**. He said He *never knew* them because their work was not according to *the will of His Father.* (Matthew 7:21-24).

Matthew 23:5 speaks of works done *to be seen of men.*

"For by grace are ye saved through faith; and that not of yourselves: it is the gift of God: Not of works, lest any man should boast." Ephesians 2:8-9

In the books of Acts and James, we see that faith and repentance come before works.

"Then said they unto him, What shall we do, that we might work the works of God? Jesus answered and said unto them, This is the work of God, that ye believe on him whom he hath sent." John 6:28-29

"that they should repent and turn to God, and do works meet for repentance (**Acts 26:20**).

"Seest thou how faith wrought with his works, and by works was faith made perfect?" James 2:22

2 Timothy 1:9 teaches us that salvation is not according to our works but *according to his purpose before the world began.*

"Who hath saved us, and called us with an holy calling, not according to our works, but according to his own purpose and grace, which was given us in Christ Jesus before the world began."

We can do nothing to save ourselves. The following verses which explain His work of righteousness for us is worth our meditation. It has been through meditation that I understand the power of God that saves us and works all His will through us. Understanding these brings the fruit of good works from the root of faith that He has planted within us.

> **"Not by works of righteousness which we have done**, but according to his mercy he saved us, by the washing of regeneration, and renewing of the Holy Ghost; Which he shed on us abundantly through Jesus Christ our Saviour; That being justified by his grace, we should be made heirs according to the hope of eternal life.
> This is a faithful saying, and these things I will that thou affirm constantly, that they which have believed in God might be careful to maintain good works. These things are good and profitable unto men." Titus 3:5-8

Ephesians 2:10 teaches that good works are God's plan—making us His workmanship in our relationship with Christ—good works that God ordained before we ever knew Him, *that we should walk in them;* that we should do them in His timing.

> "For we are his workmanship, created in Christ Jesus unto good works, which God hath before ordained that we should walk in them." Ephesians 2:10

In the following we see His workmanship in us and through us. He is the captain who begins and continues the work He has ordained for each of us.

> "Wherefore, my beloved, as ye have always obeyed, not as in my presence only, but now much more in my absence, work out your own salvation with fear and trembling.
> For it is God which worketh in you both to will and to do of his good pleasure." Philippians 2:12-13

The Will, Zeal and Skill

> "Now unto him that is able to do exceeding abundantly above all that we ask or think, according to the power that worketh in us," Ephesians 3:20

Good Works

"Now the God of peace, that brought again from the dead our Lord Jesus, that great shepherd of the sheep, through the blood of the everlasting covenant,

Make you perfect in every good work to do his will, working in you that which is well pleasing in his sight, through Jesus Christ; to whom be glory for ever and ever. Amen." Hebrews 13:20-21

"For the grace of God that bringeth salvation hath appeared to all men,
Teaching us that, denying ungodliness and worldly lusts, we should live soberly, righteously, and godly, in this present world;

Looking for that blessed hope, and the glorious appearing of the great God and our Saviour Jesus Christ;
Who gave himself for us, that he might redeem us from all iniquity, and purify unto himself a peculiar people, zealous of good works." Titus 2:14 (11-14)

Skill in the work of the Lord comes from a knowledge of Him. Paul prayed for the Colossian church that they would *be filled with wisdom and knowledge of God* for the work of the kingdom.

"That ye might walk worthy of the Lord unto all pleasing, being fruitful in every good work, and increasing in the knowledge of God;" Colossians 1:10

Our works come through wisdom and knowledge and are done in meekness.

"Who is a wise man and endued with knowledge among you? let him shew out of a good conversation his works with meekness of wisdom." James 3:13

Good works result from *faith, love, and patience of hope in our Lord.*

> "Remembering without ceasing your work of faith, and labour of love, and patience of hope in our Lord Jesus Christ, in the sight of God and our Father;" 1 Thessalonians 1:4

Good works are done in love for one another and with one another. Good works are rarely done in solitary, but as part of the whole of the body of Christ in our love and faith in Him. Faith is the root of the living Christ in us.

> "And let us consider one another to provoke unto love and to good works:" Hebrews 10:24

> "And let the beauty of the Lord be upon us and establish thou the work of our hands upon us. Yea, the work of our hands, establish thou it." Psalm 90:17

> "And he that overcometh, and keepeth my works unto the end, to him will I give power over the nations:" Revelation 2:26

From the beginning of time, from the creation, from generation to generation, we attribute all work to God. Everything accomplished in creation and redemption has been His work through His Son Jesus Christ. From the physical birth of man to spiritual birth by His Holy Spirit, all is the work of His holy will.

He worked through the prophets in the Old Testament. In the New Testament, we see how He worked through His Son to accomplish our redemption—salvation by faith in the work of Christ alone. From the new birth, to growth and maturity, to the end of this world and eternity, all is from Him and all to His glory.

> "Every man's work shall be made manifest: for the day shall declare it, because it shall be revealed by fire; and the fire shall try every man's work of what sort it is." 1 Corinthians 3:13

Dear Father in heaven, before whom we live and do all our work, we thank you for saving us by your grace that we may in your will, with the zeal of your Spirit within us, in the wisdom and knowledge of our Lord Jesus Christ, be skilled in all you have ordained for us. Let us live, be led, walk in the Spirit and rejoice to serve you now and forever. In Jesus' name, we pray. Amen.

17

Peace and Contentment

Who today can write of peace and contentment, first-hand? I originally planned this chapter for the series *Contentment* and it was the most difficult of all, so it did not make it in that series. However, we thought it would fit well as a chapter in this book. In seeking to share what I have discovered from God's Word, this may have been the one I needed the most. It is one thing to write what I have learned, second-hand, but different to share it from experience. I wanted to do more with this subject. I do not do the subject of *peace* justice. So, I pray the Lord's blessings for what we offer here.

I know the peace that is "the fruit of the Spirit" of God (**Galatians 5:22**). I can share no other peace than what God has given me through His Son, Jesus Christ (**Romans 5:1**). It has been tried and I have many times been lacking, not because I do not have peace, but because it is not a natural trait. It will always be tested while we live amid chaos.

Here, we will pose questions; and attempt to answer from the Word of the Lord.

How do peace and contentment relate to each other? There is no Biblical reference that combines these two. Since we have written much on contentment, we will document what we know of peace, seeing that the two are similar, understanding that one compliments the other. If we have the peace of God through His Son, Jesus Christ, we will be content in His peace.

The Source of Peace

The question is not "what" but "where and who is the source of peace?" Peace comes from the Lord, our God, who originally created all things for peace in His kingdom.

He is still the source and the giver of His peace.

> "The Lord lift up his countenance upon thee, and give thee peace." Numbers 6:26

> "The Lord will give strength unto his people; the Lord will bless his people with peace."
> Psalm 29:11

We are "led forth with peace." Isaiah 55:12

He has "made a covenant of peace, an everlasting covenant with His people." Ezekiel 37:26

> "He keeps in perfect peace those whose mind is stayed on Him and trusts in Him." Isaiah 26:3

> "Lord, thou wilt ordain peace for us: for thou also hast wrought all our works in us." Isaiah 26:12

He promises His people a peaceable habitation, and in sure dwellings, and in quiet resting places; Isaiah 32:18

Peace is associated with His light. Isaiah 45:7

He creates "the fruit of the lips; 'Peace.' Isaiah 57:19

He extends peace to His people "like a river," Isaiah 66:12

"For I know the thoughts that I think toward you, saith the Lord, thoughts of peace, and not of evil, to give you an expected end." Jeremiah 29:11

He reveals his "abundance of peace and truth." Jeremiah 33:6

HE IS THE **GOD OF PEACE**

"For God is not the author of confusion, but of peace." 1 Corinthians 14:33

In letters to the early churches, the apostle Paul included greetings from the God of peace. Romans 15:33, Romans 16:20, 2 Thessalonians 3:16

He is "the God of hope that fills believers with joy and peace." Romans 15:13

As the God of peace, He established the everlasting covenant through Christ. Hebrews 13:20 and sanctifies and preserves His people until Christ returns. 1 Thessalonians 5:23

PEACE OF GOD
The peace of God "rules in our hearts," Colossians 3:15

"And the peace of God, which passeth all understanding, shall keep your hearts and minds through Christ Jesus." Philippians 4:7

PEACE FROM GOD
Paul spoke of "grace and peace from God our Father, and the Lord Jesus Christ to the saints and brethren" in Romans 1:7; Colossians 1:2; 1 Corinthians 1:3; 2 Corinthians 1:2; Galatians 1:3; Ephesians 1:2; 2 Thessalonians 1:2; Titus 1:4; Philemon 1:3.

John spoke of "grace, mercy, and peace, in truth and love." 2 John 1:3

PEACE WITH GOD
There is only one reference to peace *with* God, which comes by faith, through our Lord Jesus Christ. Romans 5:1

RIGHTEOUSNESS AND PEACE
There are many references that associate peace with righteousness.

The most familiar may be Romans 17:14.

> "For the kingdom of God is not meat and drink; but righteousness, and peace, and joy in the Holy Ghost."

The Psalmist speaks of peace that comes by righteousness. Psalm 72:3

> "Righteousness and peace have kissed each other." Psalm 85:10

> "The righteous flourish; with abundance of peace." Psalm 72:7

> "And the work of righteousness shall be peace; and the effect of righteousness quietness and assurance for ever." Isaiah 32:17

And "the fruit of righteousness is sown in peace of them that make peace." James 3:18

Hebrews 12:11 says that "chastening yields the peaceable fruit of righteousness unto them which are exercised thereby."

Peace and Contentment

Paul instructs Timothy to "follow righteousness, faith, charity, peace, with them that call on the Lord out of a pure heart." 2 Timothy 2:22

WISDOM AND PEACE
Peace is the result of wisdom.

> "For length of days, and long life, and peace, shall they add to thee." Proverbs 3:2

> "Her ways are ways of pleasantness, and all her paths are peace." Proverbs 3:17

The wisdom that is from above is first pure, then peaceable. James 3:17

GOSPEL OF PEACE
Paul speaks of "our feet shod with the preparation of the gospel of peace." Ephesians 6:15 and "the feet of them that preach the gospel of peace!" Romans 10:15

GOD'S LAW AND PEACE
Those who love God's law have "great peace: and nothing shall offend them." Psalm 119:165

Great peace comes from the Lord as we are taught by Him. Isaiah 54:13

Gracious Father of grace and peace, we thank you for giving us your Son that He may bring us to you in His peace; that we may live in peace with you through Him and the power of your Holy Spirit. Fill us with your Spirit, that we may live in this peace, content with whatever you have chosen for us as you prepare us for your glory. In Jesus' name, I pray. Amen.

18

Breakthrough and Follow-Through

So as not to miss any gods they might appease, the Athenians had set up an "unknown god" among the others. And so, Christianity today is seen as a religion among many others. The God of Christianity is "unknown" even to some who claim it as their faith. If we see little more than the surface of this way of life, we simply exist without the source and the power of this life. **For the most part, we fail to differentiate between Christianity and what other religions offer.**

We must be sure that it is an offering; a supernatural offering between our God and us. It is a spiritual gift from the Lord God of Christianity whom we know as Jesus Christ, the only begotten Son of Jehovah, the Almighty God and Creator of the heavens and the earth and Redeemer of mankind.

Is There a Basic Christianity?

Baptized as a child on a profession of faith, I considered Christianity basic but ineffective in my life until as an adult, I was drawn to read, then study, to write and teach what I was learning from the Bible. During those years, the Holy Spirit I was reading about in the Bible used God's own words to transform my life. Through a new birth, with a new heart and new spirit, my life was changed and has not been the same for decades. My books, articles, and poems attest to the revealed and fulfilled promises made to those He brings to Himself.

The best way I can describe this new way of life is with a parable I heard several years ago.

A prisoner was held captive for years, not knowing where he was. He existed in an obscure stronghold in a foreign country. His food and drink were barely enough to keep him alive. Since he knew no other way of life, he did not know to wish for anything else.

One day a stranger entered his cell and told him about life outside his captivity. He had come to deliver him. At first, the man could not vision anything beyond his own existence, and so refused to follow him out. Unknown to the prisoner, the stranger had broken through the outside barrier of the stronghold to save him. He was there, not to be refused; and so, stayed with him, living off the same fare by which the prisoner had been fed most of his life.

At times he would open the cell door and lead him down a long dark hallway to show him the light outside. Not used to the light, the prisoner would soon move back to his comfortable cell.

In time, the stranger presented truths about the light, each day praying with him and leading him a little further out from his cell. Gradually getting used to the light, he was drawn more, then more, to it. One day, his eyes becoming used to the light, embraced the light, walking with the stranger into a new life outside himself.

Mission Impossible
As I contemplated writing this post, I was reminded of an old TV series *Mission Impossible*. A different mission presented to the team with every episode including the statement, "This is your mission if you choose to accept it." The missions involved seemingly impossible situations providing an escape for captives.

Breakthrough and Follow-Through

I imagined what this would have looked like for Jesus before Creation. He and the Holy Spirit were the team, Jesus, being the one who would suffer and sacrifice to bring His people out of their bondage. His mission from God the Father was to go down, go to, and live with the captives on earth; live in full obedience to God's law, which no man had ever done, and provide a true understanding of the laws of His kingdom.

He would be the light from heaven to people living in darkness, under oppression and sin. He would at the appointed time, be offered up as a means of appeasing the unknown God and ascend back to the Father, where He would live and reign for us as His people. He would send His Spirit of light from heaven; through His Word bring us out of our captivity and guide us into all truth.

Jesus accepted and fulfilled His mission. His Holy Spirit is now fulfilling His mission in our hearts and lives as we continue to follow Jesus.

Gracious Father in heaven, we praise you for so loving us that you sent your Son to be a propitiation for our sins. Lord Jesus, we thank you for being the author and finisher of our faith; for breaking through and enabling us to follow through this darkness until we see you in your full glory. Holy Spirit, we know your presence and power of the life of Christ in us. Continue to reveal and fulfill all that the Father has willed for us as your people. In Jesus' name, we pray. Amen.

19

Bound by Grace ~ Free to Love

Bound by Grace was an article I wrote thirty years ago. Here, I have added a second part–*Free to Love,* first looking at who we are when we think we are free without God, and then to the beauty and power of God's grace and liberty He gives through His Son, Jesus Christ.

As we begin this chapter, let us consider one thing first:

The Danger of Freedom
If you ask different people what it means to be free, you will get a variety of answers. For a non-believer, freedom means that they are answerable to no one, able to do whatever they want without restrictions, especially without God.

What is the danger in this kind of freedom?

Imagine intersections without traffic lights and roads without speed zones. If everybody had this freedom, who would be safe? Everyone would have the license to destroy other people who get in their way.

The danger of freedom applies to a Christian as well as a person who has no faith in Christ. Many think all men have a *free will* with the ability to choose right from wrong, even to believe or not to believe in Christ. After years of thinking I had chosen Christ as my Savior, my thinking changed. Studies in God's Word uncovered truths I had never heard.

Beginning in Genesis, I came to understand how God proved man is not capable of choosing what is right. Left to themselves, Adam and Eve showed that without the continual presence and leading of their Creator, they had no wisdom or knowledge to make the right decision. Without His presence and oversight, they had no protection from the danger in their own territory. Instead of being free, they became servants of Satan; the human race came under his bondage and except through Christ, live in rebellion against God.

Jesus, the Mediator
Jesus Christ is the mediator sent from our heavenly Father to restore us to Him—to bring us to that relationship He had planned for His Creation. Without our total dependence on Him, we will never live in true freedom.

Without Christ, we are in danger of our own deceptive thinking and without protection in this world. Satan is always waiting for us to make our own decisions without knowing or wanting God's will for us. God's will according to His law is the only free will and the only law that matters to us as His people.

Let us look now at the liberty that is given to the children of God—followers of Christ.

BOUND BY GRACE
His grace is sufficient in all of life for all He wills us to do and for all our physical needs. It is this sufficiency of the Lord, our God, *the Everlasting One, the Creator of the ends of the ear—who neither faints nor is weary.... But gives power to the faint; and to them that have no might He increases strength*—that the original article *Bound by Grace* was shared with believers thirty years ago.

Grace Revealed in Pain
It was His marvelous grace given one morning as I was in physical pain, prompting my heart to dwell on God's will and His grace. The limitation of physical movement was sometimes the only time

God could reach me—the position in which I was *prone* to listen to Him. But, oh, how wonderful were His revelations during those times and since then.

In searching the dictionary for the meanings of the word *bound*, I expected to find at least two. But I have discovered many times when I am on a treasure hunt, there is always more than I expect to find—such is the Kingdom of our Lord.

I found four meanings with other words relative to the word *bound* and even then, I could see that I could have written a whole book just from those words. We will only touch on each one as the definition relates to God's grace—remembering that *GRACE* originated with God as *unmerited and undeserved mercy and favor*.

A. BOUND n. 1. a limit.
2. The territory on or limiting lines
v.1. to limit. 2. To border on another area; adjoin.
3. To demarcate.
The word BOUNDARY is a noun defined as *something that marks a limit or border*. Webster's II New Riverside Dictionary

The picture came to mind of the lines drawn by a surveyor—lines that defined our property. They enabled us to know the limit and the borders of where we lived (not that it belonged to us—God and the bank owned the land and the house, but it was for our use and enjoyment.)

When someone or something gets too close, He shields us by His grace from the predators of the world. To allow us beyond the *BOUNDS OF GRACE* would mean that He does not care for His own children. These boundary lines prove His love and His keeping for us.

To think death or injury to one of His children is to be beyond the BOUNDS OF GRACE is to call the grace of God unjust. Like the sky, His grace is always there, working even in death, injury and difficult situations.

In any circumstance, His arms of grace can enfold and bind us even more closely to Him.

Imagine a child who falls (even within the spiritual boundaries, physical mishaps occur) and always seeks the tender—the caretaker—for comfort and for instructions against falling again. God's grace draws us to Him, as He comforts and heals.

Knowing our Limitations
As we get older, we learn our limitations and accept with respect and adoration what the experience of His grace teaches us—not to fear the things of this world, but to fear Him.

The *fear of God* alerts us to what happens when we are not submissive and obedient to the limit and border of His grace.

It is His grace to which He has bound us and that of His own doing, not ours. By His grace, He has saved us; bound us to Him through His Son, Jesus.

Without a knowledge of the truth about our heavenly Father, it is possible to *take His grace in vain* (2 Corinthians 6:1)—even testing our limits. (This is testing God—Matthew 4:7) We can be deceived if we stand on the property line and listen to someone outside our limits, but He knows the deceivers and He knows His own children, how to shield and move them.

Lines of Demarcation
The word *demarcate* means a line of solid definition with no questions. Just as a surveyor gives a paper with the lines drawn for our property, God's grace is defined by His Word, revealed by His Holy Spirit for guidance in seeing and understanding the lines set. We do not have to argue with our neighbor—within God's kingdom or in the world.

Each child within God's kingdom knows the line of demarcation. He drew the line for us in Christ at the cross. We are free in the spiritual boundaries of grace to move about in the physical world knowing what is off-limits, living daily according to the grace extended by the power of His will, wherever we are.

In Christ, God's power is ours to resist the temptations that surround us.

B. BOUND adj. 1. Confined by bonds. 2. Under obligation. 3. Enclosed in a cover or binding. 4. Certain.

There is a house on our property and within these walls, we have shelter, heat, clothing, food, and all our physical needs—according to God's grace. Without these walls, these things would deteriorate, blow away, melt, freeze, or be stolen. We require the confinement coupled with the freedom to walk in and out of the structure according to His will. The confinement is good and works for our good.

Our Obligation

This work of grace is on our behalf, but there is an obligation. We must maintain it with regular up-keep, cleaning, and repair. A house is enclosed to protect us from inclement weather and those who are not *BOUND BY GRACE*. Our faith is not in the houses that our heavenly Father provides but in Him the giver of all that we need.

God reveals His grace to us in Jesus Christ. He (God) was in Christ, reconciling the world to Himself (2 Corinthians 5:19) so He might bring us by His grace—not that we might just come back anytime we wanted to on our own but by God's grace, to be drawn to Jesus and therefore bind us to Him. He finds us and brings us to the Shepherd (John. 6:44-45, 63-65). We see the bonds in the arms of the cross and in the blood of Jesus and His love that bought us. And because He has twice owned us—by creation and by redemptive grace—we are not our own. We owe all to Him. We are under obligation to Him for our physical and eternal life.

But He does not call in a *debt* that we could never pay. We have received a statement, sealed with His own blood—*PAID*. The covering and the binding are the bountiful mercies of God with the blood that *washes whiter than snow*, and makes us His own, *sanctified and purified, holy and blameless, keeping our soul, mind, and spirit until Christ comes again* (**1 Thessalonians 5:23-24**).

BOUND BY GRACE, our sins are covered, and we are given power over sin, never desiring to be loosed from our Creator and Redeemer.

We wear *the mantle of praise* and are anointed with *the oil of gladness*. He binds us with His grace, spreading it through our whole being. We are certain that what He promises in the salvation of Jesus Christ is true—that the power of redemption works for our binding every moment of every day. He does not loose what He Himself binds to Himself. *No one can snatch us out of His hand* (**John. 10:28-29**).

Boundaries

In that house and the one in which we now live, we and our neighbors know our boundaries. Within these boundaries, there is a sense of freedom, security, and peace. We live, work, play, and invite others to enjoy the place set for us within these boundaries. God gives us in His kingdom a place much like our physical home. We, in agreement with the *surveyor,* allow God to define His spiritual bounds (boundaries) within our physical boundaries—the unseen operating in that which is seen. He sets the limits and lines border between His kingdom and the kingdom of the world. Just as the blue sky surrounds it all, His grace holds us within our spiritual boundaries and keeps the world out.

It is the grace of our heavenly Father, who in Christ came as a Savior, that defines the boundaries between His kingdom and the world and sets the standards for enjoying these bounds. Those who have submitted to these limits and borders know the freedom, security, and peace set for them in and by God's grace.

The thought came too, of keeping children within the properties where they live. Small children without knowing dangers sometimes venture beyond those limits if their caretaker is not there to restrict them from harm. It is the grace of a loving Father that keeps His eye on us at all times. Under His care and assurance, we will not go beyond our boundaries. He keeps us and limits us for our *sanctification* and *purification*—to know His holiness and His deliverance in times of temptation.

In the arms of grace, He sweeps us up and holds us when we venture too close to the boundary line (1Corinthians 10:13; 1 Thessalonians 5:23-24; Hebrews 3:20-21).

C. BOUND v. 1. To leap forward; a spring. 2. To advance by leaping. 3. To bounce.

As we are *BOUND BY GRACE*, the Spirit of God creates His own energy. Within that which we willingly surrender to Him, He is free to exercise the maximum of His grace. We are limited, but He is not. When He binds our spirit to His, something happens that we cannot explain. He creates *a new heart and a new spirit* (Ezekiel 36:26). He puts *a new song in the heart* that is bound to Him. Eternal life from the Father to the child who lives continually in His presence—*BOUND BY GRACE*—knows no limits of His power, which we will discover in the last part—Free to Love.

Gracious Father, the God of all grace, who has called us to your eternal glory through Jesus Christ our Lord, we thank you and praise you for such a precious grace that does a powerful work in our hearts and lives. Fill us with your Spirit; continue keeping us and growing us in grace and knowledge of our Lord Jesus Christ, in whose name I pray. Amen.

Free to Love
When God sent Moses to Egypt, He had a single purpose for delivering the Israelites from their bondage. Because they were like Adam and Eve in rebellion against Him, God had sent them into captivity. For seventy years they had been in slavery (the same number of years they had rebelled against God's Word in profaning the Sabbath).

It was an act of God's grace through Moses, that he led them out of Egypt to serve Him, to worship Him, to bring them into a land of promise—a new land where they would know the freedom God wanted for them.

Shortly after they were given this freedom from their hard labor, they rebelled against Moses' leadership, even asking to go back to Egypt. They did not trust God to provide for them. Neither did they worship Him according to His will.

At Mount Sinai, the multitude influenced Aaron to make a golden image and sinned in their idol-worship. They never experienced the reality of freedom. It was only the second generation that survived and entered the land of Canaan under Joshua's leadership.

The Law

The Law presented at Mount Sinai, was not written in stone for their freedom. It was God's means of showing them and future generations His kingdom of love. Through His law, He planned to bring to Himself a helpless and hopeless people who knew they could not live in full obedience to His Law.

A New Covenant

To the Hebrew Christians, the writer of Hebrews quotes the promise of a new covenant in Jeremiah 31:33 made to the house of Israel. The Law through Moses was the old covenant—the Old Testament revelation of God's kingdom. He promised to write the new covenant *in their hearts.*

> "For finding fault with them, he saith, Behold, the days come, saith the Lord, when I will make a new covenant with the house of Israel and with the house of Judah:
> Not according to the covenant that I made with their fathers in the day when I took them by the hand to lead them out of the land of Egypt; because they continued not in my covenant, and I regarded them not, saith the Lord.

For this is the covenant that I will make with the house of Israel after those days, saith the Lord; *I will put my laws into their mind, and write them in their hearts: and I will be to them a God, and they shall be to me a people:*
In that he saith, A new covenant, he hath made the first old. Now that which decayeth and waxeth old is ready to vanish away." Hebrews 8:8-10, 13

This new covenant—the New Testament revelation—is a covenant of redemption through the blood of His Son, Jesus Christ. His death was counted as the punishment for our sins—a propitiation (1 John 4:10).

God planned the sacrifice of His Son to appease His wrath and set us free from condemnation under the law and from the power of sin.

> "There is therefore now no condemnation to them which are in Christ Jesus, who walk not after the flesh, but after the Spirit.
> For the law of the Spirit of Life in Christ Jesus hath made me free from the law of sin and death.
> For what the law could not do, in that it was weak through the flesh, God sending his own Son in the likeness of sinful flesh, and for sin, condemned sin in the flesh:
> That the righteousness of the law might be fulfilled in us, who walk not after the flesh, but after the Spirit." Romans 8:1-4

The Covenant of Grace
This new covenant is the Covenant of Grace, by which He binds us to Himself and through which He delivers us from our bondage to serve Him. It is the power of the Holy Spirit that fills His people with the desire and the freedom to obey His written Law.

It is the *new heart and new spirit* that loves as God loves—a heart that loves His law (Psalm 1) and a spirit that rejoices to live in obedience to Him.

As He binds us to Him through His covenant, we are free to *love Him with all our heart, soul, mind and strength and our neighbor as ourselves*. Every hindrance has been removed that would keep us from loving Him and others.

> "Stand fast therefore in the liberty wherewith Christ hath made us free, and be not entangled again with the yoke of bondage.
>
> **For, brethren, ye have been called unto liberty; only use not liberty for an occasion to the flesh, but by love serve one another.**
> **For all the law is fulfilled in one word, even in this; Thou shalt love thy neighbour as thyself.**
> But if you are led of the Spirit, you are not under the law."
> Galatians 5:1, 13-18

Those led by *the Spirit of truth* (John 16:13) understand that the law is written in our hearts; as we *meditate on His Law*—His Word, we *hide it in our hearts* so we will *not sin against Him* (Psalm 119:11). We are not under the law but we live freely under the power of His Spirit to love Him and others; we *establish the law* (Romans 3:31) by faith in His salvation from the bondage of sin.

Dear Father in heaven, we thank you for the freedom that is ours in Christ, as you fulfill all your will in us. We praise you that you bought us by the blood of your Son. You sought us as your lost sheep, brought us to yourself, bound us by your Covenant of Grace, and taught us to live freely in love and obedience within a corrupt society. Let us love as you love—for your glory and our joy. In Jesus' name, we thank you and praise you. Amen.

20

God's Utmost for My Highest

> "Ye have seen what I did unto the Egyptians,
> and how I bare you on eagles' wings,
> and brought you unto myself."
> Exodus 19:4

When I add my comments to a familiar work, it is not to belittle the beloved author. I cut my spiritual eye-teeth on *My Utmost for His Highest*. The thought I intend here with Oswald Chambers' popular devotional is to share what the Lord has continued to show me through the years. Besides Chamber's devotional and my studying all the books that were attributed to his lectures, there has been much more from God's Word to lead me in my understanding of the difference in what is required of me and what God does in and through me.

As I continued in my desire to serve the Lord, Andrew Murray taught me how to walk. Paul taught me to run with Christ. Christ still teaches me how to be still, to wait, and to depend on Him— for He is my life.

Oswald Chambers died at the age of forty-three after complications from appendicitis. Learning this from his biography, I realized even as astute as he was in the Scriptures; he was still a student as we all are in this life. His books were written and published from the notes of his wife who attended his lectures.

Man's Inability to Obtain His Own Salvation
Teachings that turn men from trusting God for total salvation to giving part of that work into the hands of men are my point.

Growing up with this kind of thinking always left me needful and frustrated with my inability to perform the spiritual work I thought I had to do for this salvation. I loved the teachings of Chambers, whose mother was a follower of Charles Spurgeon, and I continued to desire my utmost for God. However, the more I studied the Scriptures, the more I learned of my sinful nature, my depravity, and my inability to produce anything worthy to bring to Him.

My utmost always paled compared to what I wanted to do and what I knew He expected. It fell even further below the standard when I began to learn what God promises to do for, in, and through me.

> "The Lord God is my strength,
> and he will make my feet like hinds' feet,
> and he will make me to walk upon mine high places."
> Habakkuk 3:19

The Superior Work of the Holy Spirit
When the Holy Spirit did a supernatural work in my life, apart from anything I had tried to do, ask, think, or believe, I was a new creature. With a new heart and spirit, I was able to understand His Word, His will, and His way—apart from anything I could do on my own.

Man cannot do the spiritual work required for salvation; only the power of God's Spirit within man can do what is needful for reconciliation and renewal in our relationship with Him. A dead person cannot will himself to faith and obedience. Only the power of His Holy Spirit can birth a person into His kingdom. Only as I am led, walk, and live by His Spirit can I live separated from the world, humble and holy before Him and the world.

Only a total salvation can deliver from a total depravity.

God planned His utmost for me *before the foundation of the world* (Ephesians 1:3-6; Titus 3:5) through the covenant of redemption made with His Son, Jesus Christ (2 Timothy 1:9). He sent Jesus at the time of His choosing (Galatians 4:3-9) as an utmost *sacrifice* (Hebrews 9:26) to be *a propitiation for my sins* (1 John 4:9). Even my *faith* in His working of *mercy* and *love* (Ephesians 2:4-10) is His gift of *grace*.

He convicts me of sin (John 16:8) and by His goodness brings me to repentance (Romans 2:4). Every day, He proves His utmost for my keeping *by His pow*er alone (1 Peter 1:1-5). As sanctified and the sanctifier, Jesus is *bringing many sons unto glory* (Hebrews 2:10-11) by His redemptive work alone.

> "But this man, after he had offered
> one sacrifice or sins for ever,
> sat down on the right hand of God;"
> Hebrews 10:12
> "Wherefore he is able also
> to save them to the uttermost
> that come unto God by him,
> seeing he ever liveth
> to make intercession for them."
> Hebrews 7:25
> "And this is the Father's will which hath sent me,
> that of all which he hath given me
> I should lose nothing,
> but should raise it up again at the last day."
> John 6:29

Dear Father in Heaven we are humbled that you quicken us from the dead in our trespasses and sin and accomplish your holy will in the lives of your children. Make us aware of our weakness and your power for all things pertaining to life and godliness. In Jesus' name, I pray. Amen.

21

Focus, Love, and Rejoice

The words *focus, love, and rejoice* came from my time in prayer, meditation in God's Word, and in my circumstances. The first word, *focus,* is included in the title of a book I started a few years ago. *Focus, Balance, and Order* came during a time when things were difficult to sort through. Still working on this book, I hope to finish it soon as the Lord continues to show me these three facets of Christian life.

In the meantime, the Lord placed *Focus, Love, and Rejoice* in my heart to experience the outcome of our *focus* on God our Father, the *balance* of life through our Lord, Jesus Christ and the *order* of the Holy Spirit in our lives.

It is the work of a triune God that produces the *focus, love,* and *joy* in us as His children. Briefly, let us look at this fruit that shows His work in and through us.

Focus
Concentration has never been my nature. The Lord knows my weakness and blesses me to know my need for Him—to seek His presence to accomplish in me what He desires. I would venture to say that the physical world detracts us, so we have difficulties in training our minds to look to Him for all things.

We, as earthlings, are prone to switch from image to image looking for something new, something different every day. We can easily be entertained by whatever comes in view of our senses.

The *focus* we speak of here is a steady, non-altering gaze immovable from its one object.

> "If ye then be risen with Christ,
> seek those things which are above,
> where Christ sitteth on the right hand of God."
> Colossians 3:1

He wants us to *focus* on Him. We can *love* and *rejoice* as we receive His Words by a direct concentration and meditation on Him and His Word. We receive from Him with open hearts and minds. Imagine a thirsty man holding a cup to receive water without focusing on the source. The *stream of water* is the life of Christ given to us from our heavenly Father by His Holy Spirit.

In prayer and through His Word, we direct our hearts and minds to receive the life He gives. But our eyes are on the Father, the giver of all life. Jesus directs us to the Father in His prayer on the mount.

Love and Rejoice
When He directs us to *focus, love, and rejoice*, He teaches us that *love* is the fruit, the life of Christ poured in and through us as we receive it from Him. Both *love* and *joy* are His character traits shared with His children. He gives us His *love* and His *joy*–the fruit of His Spirit within us. We, therefore, *love* as He loves, unselfishly. His joy causes us to *rejoice*.

Most will say they cannot keep such a *focus*. None of us can. Like humility and all that He requires of His children, He teaches what He wants to do in us. He gives us the desire of His heart until it becomes our heart's desire. We pray and wait for Him to do His work in us. As Andrew Murray says in Waiting on God— "we can afford to wait." These are parts of our inheritance given to enjoy here on this earth and preparation for eternity with Him.

Focus, Love, and Rejoice

When we learn to *focus* upon Him, it will not matter what may be our circumstances. *Focus* enables us to keep steadfast in the life of Christ, not changing our actions based on what is happening in and around us. The world cannot change our character when we know who we are in Christ.

We continue to *love* the unlovable and *rejoice* through the most difficult times of this life when we set our affections on Him and the things above.

Dear Father in heaven, we are most blessed when we keep our eyes heavenward, knowing you lead us through the most difficult places by your Spirit of love and joy. Bring us to desire with all our hearts to focus upon you. Make us a channel of your love and joy, we pray, In Jesus' name, Amen.

22

Living Sacrifices

> "I beseech you therefore, brethren, by the mercies of God,
> that ye present your bodies a living sacrifice,
> holy, acceptable unto God,
> which is your reasonable service."
> Romans 12:1-2

These verses in Romans 12 cannot be taken out of context but in relation to the whole letter to the Roman Church. Paul gives the means and the *reason* for His *beseeching*. Presenting our body (our whole being) is our response to *the mercies of God*. Afterward, we see the *results* of the presentation and the commitment of ourselves to Him.

The Reason

Here, Paul brings the believer to consider the truths he has presented in the previous eleven chapters. The keywords in this verse are *by the mercies of God*. Before we do anything with or for God, there has to be a revelation of Him and the work of His mercy for us.

In Romans 11:29-36, we find the capsule of God's *mercies that* opened the door—*therefore*—for Paul's beseeching the reader to consider and respond. He calls us as *brethren*—believers and followers of Christ—to bring to God the Father, the gift of His mercies in earthen vessels—for His use. When, by His mercies, He gives us *new hearts* (Ezekiel 36:26) and lives in Christ, our only reasonable response is to bring ourselves in dedication and commitment to His service and worship

Peter speaks of God's *abundant mercy* that has given us new life in Christ.

> "Blessed be the God and Father
> of our Lord Jesus Christ,
> which according to his *abundant mercy*
> hath begotten us again unto a lively hope
> by the resurrection of Jesus Christ from the dead."
> 1 Peter 1:3

A Covenant Relationship
Jesus makes us *holy and acceptable* unto God through His sacrifice for us.

Before the foundation of the world, the covenant of redemption was planned between the Father and the Son. In the power of His Holy Spirit, through the knowledge of His Word, this covenant—*the covenant of grace* as we know it—is revealed as God's plan to win us to Christ, His Son.

Betrothed to Christ
We are betrothed to Him through His sacrifice for us.
Paul's teaching in Romans 12:1-2 shows how we are to accept and enter this covenant with Him. As a wife submits to her husband in the covenant of marriage, we submit to His covenant for life here and for eternity. It is our agreement with Him that we are His temple, His building, His people, His children.

This is His means to accomplish all He desires in and through us.

> "For ye are bought with a price:
> therefore glorify God in your body,
> and in your spirit, which are God's."
> 1 Corinthians 6:20

Paul's purpose of ministry to the Gentiles was that they might *glorify God for his mercy* (Romans 15:9).

In Romans 10:3 Paul speaks of those who have not *submitted themselves* unto Him.

We must be humbled to offer ourselves as a living sacrifice. The proud cannot present themselves; *for God resisteth the proud, and giveth grace to the humble* (1 Peter 5:5-6).

> "Neither yield ye your members
> as instruments of unrighteousness unto sin:
> but yield yourselves unto God,
> as those that are alive from the dead,
> and your members as instruments
> of righteousness unto God."
> Romans 6:13

Living Sacrifices for a Living God

Paul speaks to the Thessalonians of how they *turned to God from idols to serve the living and true God;* 1 Thessalonians 1:9

> "How much more shall the blood of Christ, who through the eternal Spirit offered himself without spot to God, purge your conscience from dead works to serve *the living God?*" Hebrews 9:14

> "For he is not God of the dead, but of *the living*: for all live unto him. "Luke 20:38

> "or as much as ye are manifestly declared to be the epistle of Christ ministered by us, written not with ink, but with the Spirit of *the living God*; not in tables of stone, but in fleshy tables of the heart." 2 Corinthians 3:3

> "But ye are come unto mount Sion, and unto the city of *the living God*, the heavenly Jerusalem, and to an innumerable company of angels," Hebrews 12:22

> "But if I tarry long, that you may know how you ought to behave yourself in the house of God, which is the church of *the living God*, the pillar and ground of the truth." 1 Timothy 3:15

The Results

> "And be not conformed to this world:
> but be ye transformed
> by the renewing of your mind,
> that ye may prove what is that good,
> and acceptable, and perfect, will of God."
> Romans 12:2

When we read all of Romans 12, we find the results of the whole body of Christ living sacrificially for His glory. Except for the offering of ourselves to Him, the rest of the chapter would mean nothing to us.

When we understand the love and mercy in the sacrifice of our Lord, we willingly bring all to Him to do what He wills in and through us. He died, sacrificing all in His death for our salvation. We sacrifice all to Him to live and *prove His perfect will* in us. He performs His covenant in our lives when we enter into His covenant with Him, agreeing to His working to conform us to His image (Romans 8:29).

> "Wherefore, my brethren, ye also are become dead to the law by the body of Christ; that ye should be married to another, even to him who is raised from the dead, that we should bring forth fruit *unto God*." Romans 7:4

"Keep yourselves in the love of God, looking for the mercy of our Lord Jesus Christ unto eternal life." Jude 21

Dear Father in heaven, only you, by your Holy Spirit, can draw us to Christ. Only through your Holy Word, do we know who you are and your purpose for us. Do your holy, acceptable, and perfect will in our lives for your glory and our joy. In Jesus' name, I pray. Amen.

23

Abiding in Light and Truth

Light and Truth are the walls of the Christian faith that house the Life that is ours in the Lord Jesus Christ. Christ is the sure foundation of a living and indestructible faith (Matthew 7:24-25).

Light and ***truth*** are the work of the Holy Spirit in us and the spiritual encompassing of our heavenly Father.

Light enables us to see both physically and spiritually.

In the beginning, God, in darkness, said, "Let there be light."

> "For God, who commanded the light
> to shine out of darkness,
> hath shined in our hearts, to give the light
> of the knowledge of the glory of God
> in the face of Jesus Christ."
> 2 Corinthians 4:6

Who has done what?

God shined *THE LIGHT* in our hearts

Of the **knowledge**   **Of His glory**   **In Jesus Chris**t

What is in **THE LIGHT**? ------ **Knowledge**

Knowledge of what? -------- **The glory of God**

Where is *the glory of God* revealed? In whom is this *light* given?

In His Son, Jesus Christ

What is the purpose of *light* and *truth*?

> **"In Him was life;**
> **and his life was the light of men."**
> 1 John 1:4

> "Then spake Jesus again unto them, saying,
> I am *the light of the world*:
> he that followeth me shall not walk in darkness,
> but shall have *the light of life*."
> John 8:12

"**he that hath seen me hath seen the Father;**" (John 14:9).

His *light* and *knowledge* in us enable us to see Him and the Father.

> THE LIGHT draws us to Christ
> and keeps us in Him.
> If we live in THE LIGHT, we live in Christ.

THE LIGHT reveals THE TRUTH that is *in Christ*.

"**I am the way, the truth, and the life.**" John 14:4

Jesus was speaking of eternal life, the LIFE that He came to give. THE WAY of eternal LIFE is revealed in Christ

He is THE WAY to eternal TRUTH that leads to true LIFE.

Abiding in Light and Truth

Abiding in *Light* and *Truth* is living in Christ and Christ in us by the power of His Holy Spirit. This is a spiritual *truth* known only to God's children, children of the heavenly Father. It is a heavenly, spiritual, divine reality beyond any earthly knowledge. *Light* and *truth* do their work reflecting His *grace* and *glory* in us.

It is the *truth in* Christ by which we are *sanctified* (John17:19), *transformed* (Romans 12:2), and *conformed to* His image (Romans 8:28-29). God's written Word reveals Christ as the living Word.

> "In the beginning was the Word....with God,
> and the Word was God." John 1:1

> "And the Word became flesh and dwelt among us
> ......full of mercy and truth.
> ......grace and truth came by Jesus Christ."
> John 1:14, 17

> "Sanctify them through thy truth:
> thy word is truth."
> John 17:17

> "If ye abide in me, and my words abide in you,
> ye shall ask what ye will, and it shall be done unto you."
> John 15:7

> "He that abideth in me, and I in him,
> the same bringeth forth much fruit:
> for without me ye can do nothing."
> John 15:5

Treasury of Light and Truth
Keeping this chapter within reading limits on our blog post, I left out an important under-truth, thinking someone would read and add to what I posted. Here is the part we posted.

> "For God, who commanded the light
> to shine out of darkness,
> hath shined in our hearts, to give the light
> of the knowledge of the glory of God
> in the face of Jesus Christ."
> 2 Corinthians 4:6

Paul had mentioned in vs. 2-4 "though **by manifestation of the truth the gospel** may be hid from the lost...

> "...**the god of this world hath blinded
> the minds of them which believe not,
> lest the light of the glorious gospel of Christ,
> who is the image of God, should shine unto them.**"

Now, here is the dynamic part.

> "But we have this treasure in earthen vessels,
> that the excellency of the power may be of God,
> and not of us."
> 2 Corinthians 4:7

Through His Son, Father's LIGHT and TRUTH are given to us that we may believe. By His Word and Spirit, He alone has the power to open our minds and make Christ known in these jars of clay—It is the **excellency of His power** only that does this spiritual work in us.

Holy and Righteous Father, again I am in awe of the knowledge of your glory that is revealed in Jesus Christ. We thank you for your Holy Spirit, who continually shines this light into our hearts . Keep us abiding in Christ and your Word. Shine your light and truth through us into the darkness of thi world. In Jesus' name, I pray. Amen.

24

Preaching, Teaching, and Reaching

Week after week, Jerry and I are blessed to witness the Lord's work through the ministers of our church. This gives me much by which to express my thoughts on the Christian life that is beyond what most experience in the world today.

A mere Christianity may serve some who are independent of the church, but to see how God's Word leads His minsters to serve Him, we experience life He creates for us in the church. God's Word teaches us that we are all members of one body, with each one having its special place. Some are leaders, knowing and preaching God's Word on the Lord's Day as the center of His worship. From this Word preached, the members are given direction as to how we are to live in faith during the week. We learn how to worship at home personally and with our families, and to prepare for worship on the next Lord's Day; this all, in preparation for that eternal worship to which we live onward and upward.

PREACHING

"Therefore they that were scattered abroad went every where **preaching** the word." Acts 8:4

> "But hath in due times manifested his word through **preaching**, which is committed unto me according to the commandment of God our Saviour;" Titus 1:3

> "For the **preaching** of the cross is to them that perish foolishness; but unto us which are saved it is the power of God." 1 Corinthians 1:18

Preachers are also pastors to the Lord's sheep, knowing each family and its members.

> "And I will set up **shepherd**s over them which shall feed them: and they shall fear no more, nor be dismayed, neither shall they be lacking, saith the Lord." Jeremiah 23:4

TEACHING

But the pastor cannot do all the work. Ruling and teaching elders are ministers who teach and serve the members, reaching out beyond what the preacher is able to do.

> "And when they had ordained them elders in every church, and had prayed with fasting, they commended them to the Lord, on whom they believed." Acts 14:23

REACHING

Deacons are also servants of the Lord, knowing and attending to needs of the church.

Families and other members of the body of Christ are taught to reach out, to exhort one another; to love and teach as they are taught. Everyone prays, interceding for other members of the church. Before there is a need, a child of God knows their church family and knows where to turn; either to a close member or to a minister of the church.

It is through the body of Christ that He reaches those in need outside the church. When they see the work of Christ in us, He draws others to Him and His church.

THE TRUE CHURCH

This is the true church, growing in grace, knowledge, love and devotion to Christ and His people; knowing the Father, the Son; their presence and the power of the Holy Spirit in everyday life. Jerry and I have experienced this love and relationship with the whole of our church; blessed and praising the Lord every day for the church family He has given us.

Dear Father in heaven, we thank you that as your sheep, we have been brought into your fold under the true Shepherd who leads us in the path of righteousness for His name's sake. Thank you for placing us in the care of your under shepherds from whom we receive the truth of your Word. We are taught the doctrines of your grace; to experience heaven opened to us so that we are able to witness of Christ to others, to reach out in love when there is a need, and to praise you together for all that you are and promise to be in and through us— to your glory and our joy. In Jesus' name, we thank and praise you. Amen.

25

What is Jesus Doing in Your Life?

(Let me tell you!)

This chapter is but a synopsis of what I know of His presence and power in others and in my own life. It is worth meditation on God's Word to confirm our faith in what the Lord is doing in our lives.

Things we will speak of here:

> How Did Jesus Get into Your Life?
> What is He Doing in Your Life Now?
> Why is He in Your Life—to what end?

How Did Jesus Get into Your Life?

We sometimes make the mistake of thinking that we have chosen Jesus to be our Savior. When we read Jesus' words, we understand more than what others say about inviting Jesus into our hearts. Follow through with me to find the assurance that He gives.

As I am speaking of the supernatural presence of Jesus in the human body, soul, and spirit, I must say that Jesus did not come into my life simply by my asking Him. The process began with the Father and continued until He brought me to Himself. God, our Father revealed Jesus to me by His Holy Spirit through the knowledge of His Word. I knew *of* Him before I *knew* Him. In His timing, I understood the meaning of Ezekiel 36:26.

> "A new heart also will I give you,
> and a new spirit will I put within you:
> and I will take away the stony heart
> out of your flesh,
> and I will give you a heart of flesh."

There were those of His own people who believed Jesus when they saw His miracles and spoke the good news of the kingdom of God, but they left after He told them more about the kingdom. So, we see that they did not believe *in Christ*—they did not believe all that He said. There were things He specifically instructed those who heard His message.

> "Then Jesus said to those Jews who believed Him, ***If you*** abide in ***my word***, you are ***my disciples*** indeed." John 8:31

This quote begins with a condition and ends with an effect. We do not naturally gravitate to His Word in our natural state. The presence and power of the Holy Spirit draw us to His Word according to the will of the Father (John 6:44-45, 65-66; Galatians 1:4). The Holy Spirit that inspired the Word interprets the truths of Jesus Christ so as to bring us to repentance and faith in Him (Romans 2:4; Luke 5:32).

Even as He draws, our *abiding* in His Word is the work of His Spirit. We *abide* as He continues to lead us to read, that we may seek by the power of the Holy Spirit what He wills for us as His disciples.

The Holy Spirit reveals the Living Word (the logos, John 1), Jesus Christ, who was in the beginning: *The Word was with God and was God*. He was *made flesh to dwell among us* (John 1:14) and brings us to Him through the sacrifice of Himself—through His death, resurrection, and ascension.

Through God's Word, the Holy Spirit convicts *of sin*—our rebellion against God; *of righteousness*— and *judgment*—the judgment that is upon the world for eternity for those who do not believe and follow Him. (John 16:8-11)

What is Jesus Doing in Your Life?

Jesus told His disciples He had many things to say to them but that they *could not bear them* while He was with them.

> "Howbeit when he, the Spirit of truth, is come, he will ***guide you into all truth***, for he shall not speak of himself; but whatsoever he shall hear, that shall he speak: and he will ***shew you things to come. He shall glorify me***: for he shall receive of mine, and shall shew it unto you." John 16:12-14

It is the Holy Spirit that does the supernatural work of bringing us by faith into the Kingdom of our Lord Jesus Christ.

We did not birth ourselves naturally into this world nor do we birth ourselves spiritually into the kingdom of heaven. Any interest in Jesus Christ and the things of God begin with the new birth (John 3:3-8).

The new birth is not by our free will but by the will of God as we spoke earlier of the new heart and spirit.

> "Which were *born*, not of blood, nor of the will of the flesh, nor of the will of man, but *of God.*" John 1:13

To fully understand everything God wants for us, we must continually read His Word as the Spirit reveals more and more of Jesus, the Living Word that dwells within us.

> **"Even the Spirit of truth;**
> **whom the world cannot receive,**
> **because it seeth him not, neither knoweth him:**
> **but ye know him; for he dwelleth with you,**
> **and shall be in you."** John 14:17

"He has ***made us in Christ to be partakers of the inheritance of the saints in light***.

Who hath ***delivered us from the power of darkness*** and hath ***translated us into the kingdom of his dear Son***: Colossians 1:12-13

"Though we were alienated from God and enemies, *yet* ***now hath he reconciled***. Colossians 1:21

"In whom we have **redemption through his blood, the forgiveness of sins**, *according to the riches of* **his grace;** Wherein *he hath* **abounded toward us in all wisdom and prudence;**" Ephesians 1:7-8

What is He Doing in Your Life Now?

> **For it is God which worketh in you both to will and to do of his good pleasure.**
> Philippians 2:13

Jesus' disciples were sorrowful at the news that He would be returning to the Father and sending His Holy Spirit in His stead (John 16:4-7). They were a privileged few among whom Jesus lived and taught—those who afterward recorded what He taught, and then spread the knowledge of Jesus, the Living Word.

The more we know of Jesus, the more we know what He is doing in us. Continuing (abiding) in His Word convinces us He is abiding in us, transforming our minds, and conforming us to His image.

> **"I am come that they might have ife, and that they might have it more abundantly."**
> John 10:10

I have often thought of the difference in Jesus and Superman. Superman, an imaginary character of a man's creation, changes from a mild-mannered reporter to a superhero. He flies down into the dire circumstances, scoops up the person in danger, returns them to their original state, and goes back to his newsroom, undetected. He has no personal relationship with those he saves.

Jesus, however, not only knows our need for salvation but also reveals Himself as the Savior. He knows each of us by name. He saves us, lives with us by His Spirit and Word—to love, care, and share His kingdom with us forever.

He is preparing us for eternity with Him.

As we wait, we *grow in grace and knowledge of Him* (2 Peter 3:12-18).

Continuing through His Word, we read how He enables us to live in the world, separate and sanctified for His use and as a light to others of His saving grace.

God the Father has given us His Word through His Son.

The following is only part of Jesus' high-priestly prayer (John 17) for His people which we do well to learn. We must meditate on what He purposes to do for us and in us.

He speaks of those who have believed that the Father sent Him (vs. 8) *for them—not for the world* (vs. 9).

Believers belong to Him and the Father; **Jesus is *glorified in them*** (vs. 10).

His *joy would be fulfilled in them* (vs.13), *He gave them the Father's word, and the world hated them, because they are not of the world, even as I am not of the world.*
We are **kept from the evil, sanctified through His Word**; *His Word is truth* (vs.15-17).

"I pray not that thou shouldest take them out of the world, but that thou shouldest ***keep them from the evil***." (vs. 15)

Jesus sanctified Himself that they also might be **sanctified through the truth** (vs. 19).

Jesus did not pray for them alone, *but for them also which shall believe on me through their word;* (vs. 20).

> "That they all may be one; as thou, Father, art in me, and I in thee, that they also may be one in us: that the world may believe that thou hast sent me (vs. 21).

> "And I have declared unto them thy name, and will declare it: that **the love wherewith thou hast loved me may be in them, and I in them**" (vs. 26).

Paul described the work of Jesus on our behalf.

> **Who gave himself for our sins,
> that he might *deliver us from this present evil world*,
> according to the will of God and our Father:**
> Galatians 1:4

Filled and Fruitful

Paul spoke to the Philippians of *being* **filled with the fruits of righteousness**, which are by Jesus Christ, **unto the glory and praise of God**. Philippians 1:11

> "Which is come unto you, as it is in all the world; and **bringeth forth fruit**, as it doth also in you, since the day ye heard of it, and knew *the grace of God in truth*." Colossians 1:6

Paul prayed for the Colossian church that they *might be* **filled with the knowledge of his will in all wisdom and spiritual understanding.**

What is Jesus Doing in Your Life?

That ye might *walk worthy of the Lord unto all pleasing, being* **fruitful n every good work, and increasing in the knowledge of God;**
Strengthened *with all might,* **according to his glorious power,** *unto all patience and longsuffering with joyfulness;* Colossians 1:9-11

"These things I have spoken unto you, that in me ye **might have peace.** n the world ye shall have tribulation: but be of good cheer; I have overcome the world." John 16:32

Strengthened, Rooted and Grounded in Love

"That he would grant you, according to the riches of his glory, to be **strengthened with might by his Spirit in the inner man;**

That Christ may dwell in your hearts by faith; that ye, being **rooted and grounded in love**, may be able to comprehend with all saints what is the breadth, and length, and depth, and height;

And to know the love of Christ, which passeth knowledge, that ye might be **filled with all the fulness of God**." Ephesians 3:16-19

Transformed and Conformed to His Image

We are being transformed from glory to glory (2 Corinthians 3:18; Romans 12:1-2) and conformed to His image (Romans 8:28-29)

"These things I have spoken unto you, that in me **ye might have peace. In the world ye shall have tribulation: but be of good cheer; I have overcome the world.** John 16:32

Why is He in Your Life—to What End?

> "That he might ***sanctify and cleanse*** *it* (the church—His people) ***with the washing of water by the word,*** That he might ***present it to himself a glorious church, not having spot, or wrinkle***, or any such thing; but that it should be ***holy and without blemish.***" Ephesians 5:26-27

To present us holy and unblameable and unreproveable in his sight: Colossians 1:22

He is ***working in us what is well-pleasing in His sight through Jesus Christ*** (Hebrews 13:29-21).

"to ***keep you from falling***, and to ***present you faultless before the presence of his glory with exceeding joy***," Jude 24

> "That in the dispensation of the fulness of times he might ***gather together in one all things in Christ***, both which are in heaven, and which are on earth; even in him:" Ephesians 1:10

"Being confident of this very thing,
that he which hath begun a good work in you
will perform it until the day of Jesus Christ:"
Philippians 1:6

"Now unto him that is able to do exceeding abundantly
above all that we ask or think,
according to the power that worketh in us,"
Ephesians 3:20

We can never in one chapter of a book present a full answer to the questions we have asked. As we pray and continue in His Word, He will reveal more, bringing us closer to Him, beyond anything we have known (Jeremiah 33:3).

Gracious Father in heaven, we do not deserve the life you have given us in Christ. We thank you and praise you for your Word and for sending your Holy Spirit to draw us to Christ. Fill us with your fullness that we may bear the fruit of righteousness for your kingdom and your glory. In Jesus' name, I pray. Amen.

26

Riveted and Radical

R & R, an abbreviation for "rest and relaxation," is the end to which most spend their lives. For those devoted to Christ—desiring the most from our relationship with Him in this life and for eternity—R & R means more than time out from our normal labors. Our calling and our work for His kingdom here on earth require a complete and indisputable loyalty to Him.

We know what rest and relaxation look like. Everyone works for it and welcomes it. It requires a total giving of ourselves to nothing but our own desires.

But there is a rest beyond this world—beyond a mere Christianity—promised to the followers of Christ even before this life is finished. We are in preparation for that eternal rest while engaged in the work of the kingdom, here.

The meaning of *rivet* (Merriam-Webster) A rivet is a fastener that holds something closed or down, and something riveting keeps you glued to your seat and grabs your attention; having the power to fix the attention; engrossing, fascinating.

To be riveted (Cambridge English Dictionary) To not be able to stop looking at something because it is so interesting or frightening.

> "For the love of Christ compels us…..that those who live should live no longer for themselves, but for Him who died for them and rose again.

> Therefore, if anyone is in Christ, he is a new creation; old things have passed away; behold, all things have become new." 2 Corinthians 5:15-17

A radical Christianity is a life no one understands except those who know Christ as Lord and Master of all life—both physical and spiritual. It is a calling by the power of the Holy Spirit for us to leave our nets and our collections to follow Him.

It is the Spirit of Jesus Christ that captures our attention even as He embraces our hearts, our minds, and our beings. I use the plural pronoun because I know I am not the only one He has chosen to follow Him.

> "Who hath also sealed us, and given the earnest of the Spirit in our hearts." 2 Corinthians 1:22 (See also Ephesians 1:13)

To engage in the profundity of the gospel of our Lord Jesus Christ means more than we can imagine. It is a spiritual, divine, and supernatural way of life. This means that He, by His Spirit, has turned my life from self—total denial to the world—to undenied sacrifice to Him.

> **"The words of the wise are as goads,**
> **and as nails fastened**
> **by the masters of assemblies,**
> **which are given from one shepherd."**
> Ecclesiastes 12:11

To be radical for Christ, we must first be riveted *to* Him—not just our eyes riveted *on* Him.

> "He that loveth father or mother more than me is not worthy of me: and he that loveth son or daughter more than me is not worthy of me." Matthew 10:37

Riveted and Radical

"Verily I say unto you, There is no man that hath left house, or brethren, or sisters, or father, or mother, or wife, or children, or lands, for my sake, and the gospel's,
But he shall receive an hundred fold now in this time, houses, and brethren, and sisters, and mothers, and children, and lands, with persecutions, and in the world to come eternal life." Mark 10:29-30

Besides the good things, persecutions are promised in this life to those who are true disciples. We will consider suffering and persecution in the Christian life in the next chapter.

When Jesus said, "If any man will come after me, let him deny himself, and take up his cross daily, and follow me" (Luke 9:23), He was using His conditional statement that begins with the word "if"—relating a difference in the ordinary and the profound—in the common and uncommon.

Even as in John 8:31-32, He was presenting the difference of a mere existence and the radical life seen in Him and His disciples. In my early Christian life, I used to pray that the Lord would "love me to death" so that He might "love me to life." He has been doing this for over twenty years—drawing me closer and closer to Him.

> "A follower of Christ is radically oriented to a different world."

Dr. Charley Chase wrote these words, knowing the content of John 6, one of the three longest chapters in the New Testament.

Reading, studying, meditation, and memorization of the undiluted truth of Jesus' teachings will either turn us away or draw us to Him forever.

Those who stay riveted to Him—not just to His teaching—will be new creatures, following and living the true life of a Christian, not for this world, but for the next (Galatians 6:14-15).

True Disciples

During the three years of His earthly ministry, many followed Jesus for the food and the healing. But they could not accept His preaching and teaching and were no longer interested in Him.

When these left, Jesus asked the twelve. "Do you also want to go away?"

> "But Simon Peter answered Him, "Lord, to whom shall we go? You have the words of eternal life. Also, we have come to believe and know that You are the Christ, the Son of the living God." John 6:67-69

Eleven of the twelve remained and after His resurrection and ascension continued His teachings and preaching of the gospel that we have today. We still have it, and like those few, there are few today who believe by the power of His Spirit and are riveted to Him, living a radical life in the face of adversity. Those who follow Christ live in light of the eternal life promised to those who are truly His disciples.

The religious leaders spoke of the apostles as "These that have turned the world upside down" (Acts 17:6).

How did they do this? It was not by their own knowledge, authority or power.

> "The Lord has appeared of old to me, saying: "Yes, I have loved you with an everlasting love; Therefore, with lovingkindness I have drawn you." Jeremiah 31:3

> "No one can come to Me unless the Father who sent Me draws him; and I will raise him up at the last day." John 6:44

> "And I, if I am lifted up from the earth, will draw all *peoples* to Myself." John 12:32

"Assemble yourselves and come; Draw near together, You who have escaped from the nations. They have no knowledge, who carry the wood of their carved image, And pray to a god that cannot save." Isaiah 45:20

The words of the wise are as goads, and as nails fastened by the masters of assemblies, which are given from one shepherd. Jesus sent Paul in ministry to the Gentiles.

"To open their eyes, and to turn them from darkness to light, and from the power of Satan unto God, that they may receive forgiveness of sins, and inheritance among them which are sanctified by faith that is in me." Acts 26:18

The same light given to Paul accompanied him wherever he went.

Seek, See, and Set your Mind on Him

"So I have looked for You in the sanctuary, To see Your power and Your glory." Psalm 63:2

"Turn away my eyes from looking at worthless things, And revive me in Your way." Psalm 119:37

"And this is the will of him that sent me, that every one which seeth the Son, and believeth on him, may have everlasting life: and I will raise him up at the last day." John 6:40

"If then you were raised with Christ, seek those things which are above, where Christ is, sitting at the right hand of God. Set your mind on things above, not on things on the earth. For you died, and your life is hidden with Christ in God." Colossians 3:1-3

We swim upstream against the current of this world—meeting and warning those on the path to destruction.

"For those who live according to the flesh set their minds on the things of the flesh, but those who live according to the Spirit, the things of the Spirit." Romans 8:5

"And ye shall seek me, and find me, when ye shall search for me with all your heart." Jeremiah 29:13

> **"To the end he may stablish your hearts
> unblameable in holiness before God,
> even our Father,
> at the coming of our Lord Jesus Christ
> with all his saints."**
> 1 Thessalonians 3:13

Dear Father in heaven, your greatness is unsearchable. You have made the gospel of our Lord Jesus Christ more powerful than we will ever know. By your Spirit you call us, you draw us by your grace; you turn us so we may look, gaze and wonder at your Son. You have lifted Him through death and resurrection to sit at your right hand, to rule and govern a people for yourself, to call in each generation those who will give all to live for you. As we live in obedience of the living faith you have given us, display in us the same diligence and fervency of our Lord that sets us apart from this world that it may be turned upside down. In Jesus' name, I pray. Amen.

27

Nailing our Theses

What do we know of the background of the Christian faith? Without knowing the history of the church, we know nothing of what some have gone through to preserve our faith. Here, we will look briefly at the Reformation in the 1500s through the work of Martin Luther.

We have Bibles that were not available before the Reformation. The Word of God, proclaimed to all men, was held in trust by only a few of the church. That was changed when the heart and life of a young monk named Martin Luther was changed. He saw the only hope of salvation apart from works as he searched the Scriptures for himself. His study of Paul's letter to the Romans brought him to see and know Christ as his personal Lord and Savior. To make known his thoughts on the corruption of the church, he arranged his 95 theses and nailed them to the door of the church in Wittenberg, Germany, thinking to arrange discussions or debate.

> "But why October 31? November 1 held a special place in the church calendar as All Saints' Day. On November 1, 1517, a massive exhibit of newly acquired relics would be on display at Wittenberg, Luther's home city. Pilgrims would come from all over, genuflect before the relics, and take hundreds, if not thousands, of years off time in purgatory. Luther's soul grew even more vexed.

None of this seemed right. One of Luther's 95 Theses simply declares, "The Church's true treasure is the gospel of Jesus Christ. That alone is the meaning of Reformation Day. The church had lost sight of the gospel because it had long ago papered over the pages of God's Word with layer upon layer of tradition. Tradition always brings about systems of works, of earning your way back to God. It was true of the Pharisees, and it was true of medieval Roman Catholicism. Didn't Christ Himself say, "My yoke is easy and my burden is light?" Reformation Day celebrates the joyful beauty of the liberating gospel of Jesus Christ." What is Reformation Day?

"Martin Luther claimed that what distinguished him from previous reformers was while they attacked corruption in the life of the church, he went to the theological root of the problem—the perversion of the church's doctrine of redemption and grace. Luther, a pastor and professor at the University of Wittenberg, deplored the entanglement of God's free gift of grace in a complex system of indulgences and good works. In his Ninety-five Theses, he attacked the indulgence system." Reformation, *Encyclopedia Brittanica*

We might ask, "Are there false teachings in the church today?" How far have we come even in this century, from the simplicity that is in Christ, having added our own traditions, programs, etc.?

Two main questions we are led to ask at this point in the life of the church are really personal. The church will not stand in final judgment with us. We will stand alone, either in Christ through the salvation offered to us through Him, or outside of the gospel, alone and without hope for eternity.

1. What is our personal thesis? What do we believe of Christ as revealed in God's Word? Have we discovered the truths about our own salvation as Martin Luther did?

2. Where have we nailed our theses? On what doors of our lives have we proclaimed Christ as our Lord and Savior?

We have the Bible. We hold the truth in our own hands. We claim the gospel alone as our attack against false teachings and against Satan's power in the church and in our own lives.

The Door of our Hearts
We nail our beliefs to the door of our hearts. We proclaim the truths of God's grace and salvation in Christ alone, nailing these to the door of our homes, the door of our cars, the door of our workplaces, the door of our schools.

Wherever we are, as faithful followers of Christ, we wear our theses as our armor of faith, we take them wherever we go; we testify of them without fear and die with them if need be.

Are there enough of us as *living sacrifices* (Romans 12:1-2) to challenge our churches today? We must take the time to establish the truths of God's Word for ourselves, and to stand firm on His Word no matter the cost? (See Chapter 22 ***Living Sacrifices***.)

Gracious Father in heaven, thank you for leading the Reformers to know your Word and to stand firm. Thank you for those who died that we might have your Word in this generation. Guide your people to take a stand for the truth of the gospel in our churches and before the world. In Jesus' name, I pray. Amen

28

The Secret Place

The secret place of which we write is basically "the secret place of the Most High" referenced in Psalm 90:1. "He that dwells in the secret place of the Most High shall abide under the shadow of the Almighty." But it has a deeper meaning as we will show in this chapter.

How do we get to this secret place? We must first know about it through the revelation of God's Word (1 Corinthians 2). We must be born into it by His Spirit (John 3:3-8; John 1:12). It is a spiritual experience of our heart and spirit ~ He gives us a new heart and a new spirit (Ezekiel 36:26). He makes us joint-heirs with His Son in His kingdom (Romans 8:17).

He has provided the means of communication with Him in this secret place. He speaks to us through His Word and receives our speech through prayer. His Word teaches us how to pray and and how He hears our prayers and our praises. As children, we are disciples and servants of His Son Jesus Christ; God gave Him for us as a propitiation for our sins showing His great love for us (1 John 4:10). Because we are believers and His followers, we will experience a taste of His persecution from those who do not believe in Him. We experience affliction, suffering, and tribulation for His name's sake.

In Acts 5:41; the apostles left those who had beaten them, commanding their silence of the gospel, "rejoicing that they were counted worthy to suffer shame for His name.".

The Secret Place is an honorable place for His people who in all generations follow Christ—and if need be, suffer persecution.

No other people can claim this honor except those who belong to Him through His Son, Jesus Christ. As we look at the remainder of our references, I encourage you to take time to meditate on these, take them to heart and remember whose we are as pilgrims and strangers in a foreign land. If you don't have time to read all the references now, I encourage you to come back to them.

We will look at these three areas and end with a section on Chastisement:

AFFLICTION **of Christ**
AFFLICTION **of Followers of Christ**
AFFLICTION **within the Body of Christ**

AFFLICTION of CHRIST

H6031 ânâh, *aw-naw' to* afflict, oppress, humble

The ***affliction*** of Christ prophesied in Isaiah is the same word used for other references in the Old Testament.

"Surely he hath borne our griefs, and carried our sorrows: yet we did esteem him stricken, smitten of God, and ***afflicted.***" Isaiah 53:4

"He was oppressed, and he was ***afflicted***, yet he opened not his mouth: he is brought as a lamb to the slaughter, and as a sheep before her shearers is dumb, so he openeth not his mouth." Isaiah 53:7

The prophecy was fulfilled at the end of Jesus' ministry when by His affliction, He took upon Himself our punishment for sin. We are not exempt from afflictions in this life but saved from the afflictions that will come to those who do not accept His sacrifice for salvation.

In the following verses from God's Word, we hope to prove that afflictions are part of this life for all humanity because we live in a fallen, sinful world. The afflictions of unbelievers are just a prelude to the forever tune of eternal suffering. But as believers, we accept affliction as a part of our unity with Christ, our Lord, and Savior. We follow Him in the paths of righteousness with the promise that He is with us in our suffering for the sake of the gospel.

The prophecy of Jesus' sufferings bridges the gap between the Old and New Testaments, bringing us to the record of His life and HIs instructions to His disciples as He was preparing them for His crucifixion and resurrection.

"Then shall they deliver you up to be **afflicted**, and shall kill you: and ye shall be hated of all nations for my name's sake."Matthew 24:9

New Testament G2347
Strong's defines **affliction** thlipsis **thlē'-psēs** tribulation, affliction, anguish, persecution

The word is the same used for **tribulation.**

Jesus spoke of the tribulations that would come with discipleship. His encouragement was for peace and joy through His victory over death and the world. He promises all the physical blessings, including persecution (Mark 20:30).

"These things I have spoken unto you, that in me ye might have peace. In the world ye shall have *tribulation*: but be of good cheer; I have overcome the world." John 16:33

"He that spared not his own Son, but delivered him up for us all, how shall he not with him also freely give us all things?" Romans 8:32

AFFLICTION of Followers of Christ
Paul wrote of this tribulation to the early church.

"Confirming the souls of the disciples, and exhorting them to continue in the faith, and that we must through much *tribulation* enter into the kingdom of God." Acts 14:22

To the disciples in the church in Rome, Paul wrote to encourage them during those times. See how many times "joy" is related to affliction in these verses.

"And not only so, but we glory in *tribulations* also: knowing that *tribulation* worketh patience;" Romans 5:3

"Who shall separate us from the love of Christ? shall *tribulation*, or distress, or persecution, or famine, or nakedness, or peril, or sword?" Romans 8:3

"Rejoicing in hope; patient in *tribulation*; continuing instant in prayer;" Romans 12:12

"For our light *affliction*, which is but for a moment, worketh for us a far more exceeding and eternal weight of glory;" 2 Corinthians 4:17

"How that in a great trial of **affliction** the abundance of their joy and their deep poverty abounded unto the riches of their liberality." 2 Corinthians 8:2

"Who now rejoice in my sufferings for you, and fill up that which is behind of the **afflictions of Christ** in my flesh for his body's sake, which is the church:" Colossians 1:24

"And ye became followers of us, and of the Lord, having received the word in much **affliction**, with joy of the Holy Ghost." 1 Thessalonians 1:6

G3804 pathema *path'-ay-mah* from a presumed derivative of 3806; something undergone, i.e. hardship or pain; subjectively, an emotion or influence:– affection, affliction, motion, suffering. The sufferings of Christ; also the afflictions which Christians must undergo in behalf of the same cause which Christ patiently endured.

"That I may know him, and the power of his resurrection, and the fellowship of **his sufferings**, being made conformable unto his death;" Philippians 3:10

"But we see Jesus, who was made a little lower than the angels for the **suffering** of death, crowned with glory and honour; that he by the grace of God should taste death for every man." Hebrews 2:9

"Searching what, or what manner of time the Spirit of Christ which was in them did signify, when it testified beforehand the **sufferings of Christ**, and the glory that should follow." 1 Peter 1:11

"But rejoice, inasmuch as ye are partakers of partakers of *Christ's sufferings*; that, when his glory shall be revealed, ye may be glad also with exceeding joy." 1 Peter 4;13

"The elders which are among you I exhort, who am also an elder, and a witness of the *sufferings of Christ*, and also a partaker of the glory that shall be revealed:" 1 Peter 5:1

"For I reckon that the *sufferings* of this present time are not worthy to be compared with the glory which shall be revealed in us." Romans 8:18

AFFLICTION within the body of Christ

G2347 *thlipsi*s is the same word used for tribulation and *trouble* in 2 Corinthians 1:4

"Who comforteth us in all our *tribulation*, that we may be able to comfort them which are in any *trouble*, by the comfort wherewith we ourselves are comforted of God."

"For as the *sufferings of Christ* abound in us, so our consolation also aboundeth by Christ." 2 Corinthians 1:5

"And whether we be *afflicted*, it is for your consolation and salvation, which is effectual in the enduring of the same sufferings which we also suffer: or whether we be comforted, it is for your consolation and salvation." 2 Corinthians 1:6

"So that we ourselves glory in you in the churches of God for your patience and faith in all your persecutions and *tribulations* that ye endure:" 2 Thessalonians 1:4

The Secret Place

"Partly, whilst ye were made a gazingstock both by reproaches and *afflictions*; and partly, whilst ye became companions of them that were so used." Hebrews 10:33

G4778. sugkakoucheo *soong-kak-oo-kheh'-o* from 4862 and 2558; to maltreat in company with, i.e. (passively) endure persecution together: –suffer affliction with.

The writer of Hebrews speaks of Moses choosing *rather to suffer affliction with the people of God than to enjoy the pleasures of sin for a season.* Hebrews 11:25

In James 5:10 he speaks of the prophets who were *an example of suffering affliction, and of patience* ~ *New Testament Greek meaning* -- *from* G2552 kakopatheia *kak-op-ath'-i-ah* from a compound of 2256 and 3806; hardship:–suffering affliction.

In 1 Peter 4:14 we read: "If ye be reproached for the name of Christ, happy are ye; for the spirit of glory and of God resteth upon you." Is this not the "secret place" in which we dwell with Him "under the shadow of the Almighty" who has *sanctified* us and is *bringing us to glory* in Him (Hebrews 2:10-11)?

Chastisement ~ the Secret Place in the Life of God's Child

"But he was wounded for our transgressions, he was bruised for our iniquities: the chastisement of our peace was upon him; and with his stripes we are healed." Isaiah 53:5

"Though he was a Son, yet learned he obedience by the things which he suffered;" Hebrews 5:8

It was interesting that I was writing about this secret place of affliction at the same our pastor was preaching through the book of Hebrews. Finishing the eleventh chapter with the list of martyrs, we were then in Hebrews 12, seeing the relationship between God and His children, the same kind of relationship between Him and the Israelites in the Old Testament. The Old Testament speaks not only of affliction but also of chastisement (Isaiah 26:16). While we might not like the idea that He afflicted His people because of their rebellion, we might also not hold to the idea that God causes pain to His children who fail to hear and obey the instructions of His Word.

In hearing these sermons, I have been moved to a deeper understanding of what it means to be a child of God, to be blessed that He chastens me because He loves me. (Hebrews 12:5-14) and all this, so that I stay close to Him and partake of His holiness; which means I pray even for His chastisement, along with instructions and corrections as needed, so that I know Jesus did not bear my chastisement in vain but is my example in His suffering and obedience. Our chastisement fell upon Him, so that we may become the children of God.

Any pain we have to suffer now will be worth it all for the glory that waits with Him in eternity. All pain and adversity, whether or not we are suffering for Christ's sake, is accepted because the Lord our God is sovereign over all things.

"He that spareth his rod hateth his son: but he that loveth him chasteneth him betimes." Proverbs 13:5

"And he said to me, These are they which came out of great ***tribulation***, and have washed their robes, and made them white in the blood of the Lamb." Revelation 7:14

Gracious Father, we thank you for revealing the truth of your Word to us by your Holy Spirit. Enable us to accept all things, pain, sickness, and all adversity at your hand, working for our good and conforming us to the image of Christ, as we continue to abide in your word and under the shadow of your wings. Thank you for that secret place you prepared for us in Christ our Lord, in whose name I pray. Amen.

29

Striving and Surviving

To get to the depth of this chapter has been tedious. Even as I came to this, it seemed as if facing one of those brick walls we run into close to the end of a project. There is something we can't get over, around, under, or through.

I have described this overwhelming sense in other posts as finding more than I know how to handle. It is what I imagine winning the lottery would be like, only this is a spiritual windfall every time the Lord brings me to a new chapter in my life or to finishing a book.

Proving truth by our experience seems the easiest to write, but much of the time, it is His working in us what we have not yet known while we write. It is to find the joy of His presence, as He continues to teach and prepare us for eternity with Him. We live the Christian life in the presence and power of the Lord God Almighty who brings us to imagine what is beyond where we are.

From Striving to Surviving
As we grow in our faith, we go from striving to surviving and finally, thriving in the middle of the common adversities that assail all human beings. As Christians, we face the controversies that exist between believers and unbelievers as well as among God's people.

If we have come this far in this book, we know that Christianity is not a **two-bit** religion or one by which we **hitch our wagon to a star** and hope it will carry us to heaven. It is not like any other religion but one that most people seem to be happy without.

Since the beginning, when God created a man and a woman, there has been an antithesis—Satan and his angels gathering those who are captive to him to battle against God and His plan for His creation.

Persecution

The Christian life is not an easy one. The more we claim the promise of eternal life in Him, the more we are ridiculed and persecuted.

As the apostle Paul expressed the life of Jesus' disciples, "We are accounted as sheep for the slaughter." Jesus said, "If any man will come after me, let him deny himself, and take up his cross daily," Luke 9:23

Although I have not come to the point of thriving as I desire, Jerry and I have survived—experiencing joy and praise through much hardship. The vision is put before us when we study the life of Christ our Lord and the apostles who were chosen to continue His ministry of proclaiming the kingdom of God.

If we never catch sight of the victory Jesus gained for us in this world, then we believe in vain.

It is a victory of faith to overcome as He rules in every area of our lives, whether personal or relational. We need His presence and power to overcome that which makes us captive to this world.

He bought us and brought us from being an enemy, to serve Him as a soldier of the cross. He gives us every weapon in His arsenal to overcome the enemies that strive against Him and His kingdom here on earth (2 Corinthians 10:4-5).

Striving and Surviving

Our growth and survival in this world begin by knowing who and where we are. In John's first letter, he describes the difference in God's people and the world that "lies in wickedness."

"And we know that we are **of God**, and the whole world <u>lieth in wickedness</u>." 1 John 5:19

"We know that we are **of God**, and the whole world <u>lies *under the sway of* the wicked one</u>." NKJV

"We know that we are **from God**, and the whole world <u>lies in the power of the evil one</u>." ESV

"We know that we are **children of God**, and that the whole world <u>is under the control of the evil one</u>." NIV

In this one verse, we see the opposing forces of the antithesis since the world began.

KJV and NKJV agree that "we are **of** God."

ESV states "we are **from** God."

NIV says "we are **children of** God."

As disciples of Christ we belong to God, which makes us different from the world.

In the next part of this sentence, John describes those who are not children of God. Every translation describes the territory of unbelievers as "the whole world."

KJV says "the whole world **lieth in wickedness**."

NKJV says "the whole world **lies under the sway of the wicked one**.

ESV says, "the whole world **lies in the power of the evil one**.

NIV says, "the whole world is **under the control of the evil one**."

2 Corinthians 4:4 describes the evil one as **"the god of this world."**

Ephesians 2:2 describes him as **"the prince of the power of the air."**

"In this the children of God are manifest, and the children of the devil: whosoever doeth not **righteous**ness is not of God, neither he that loveth not his brother." 1 John 3:10

"Blessed is the man that walketh not in the counsel of the ungodly, nor standeth in the way of **sinners**, nor sitteth in the seat of the scornful.
But his delight is in the **law of the Lord**; and in his law doth he meditate day and night.
For the Lord knoweth the way of the **righteous**: but the way of the **ungodly** shall perish." Psalm 1:1-2, 6

"And Pharaoh sent, and called for Moses and Aaron, and said unto them, I have sinned this time: the Lord is **righteous**, and I and my people are **wicked**." Exodus 9:27

Satan's Territory
During wartimes, we hear of servicemen being taken captive as prisoners of war. Everyone since Adam and Eve, are born slaves into Satan's territory. As *the god of this world*, he rules with power over *the whole world*. A mere Christianity is not enough to survive the spiritual battles that come. A **little faith** will not stand against the vicious onslaught of the enemy. Those who do not know Christ are destined to a final eternity with Satan and his angels.

Striving and Surviving

Only Jesus Christ can save us from the enemy—the spirit of this world and his oppression.

> **"Who gave himself for our sins,
> that he might deliver us from this present evil world,
> according to the will of God and our Father."**
> Galatians 1:4

Christ's disciples are born again spiritually to belong to Him—predestined to eternity with Him. It is Jesus Christ who delivers us from the power of the evil one.

"We know that whosoever is born of God sinneth not; but he that is begotten of God keepeth himself, and that wicked one toucheth him not." 1 John 5:18

"Whatsoever is born of God overcometh the world: and this is the victory that overcometh the world, even our faith. Who is he that overcometh the world, but he that believeth that Jesus is the Son of God?" 1 John 5:4-5

"Ye are of God, little children, and have overcome them: because greater is he that is in you, than he that is in the world." 1 John 4:4

Titus 2:12 speaks of how God's children are to live in this present world.

"And that ye put on the new man, which after God is created in **righteous**ness and true holiness." Ephesians 4:24

The Power of the Holy Spirit
The Lord promises His people the power of His Holy Spirit—the same power that was with Him on earth. The same Holy Spirit by which Jesus was conceived of the virgin Mary is the same Spirit

by which Christ is born in us—the same power to overcome sin and make us holy. The same presence with Jesus as He endured the suffering and death of the cross is the same presence of the Spirit of Christ within us—to live sacrificially for Him.

It is the same power that raised Him from the dead and made Him to sit in heavenly places to rule at the right hand of the Father (Ephesians 1:19-21; Ephesians 2:5).

It is the same power given to those in persecution:

"Who through faith subdued kingdoms, wrought **righteous**ness, obtained promises, stopped the mouths of lions." Hebrews 11:33

God has chosen us before the foundation of the world (Ephesians 1:3), birthed us into His kingdom and called us for a battle against the god of this world. The purpose as children of God is not to take over this world. The Father's plan is for *a new heaven and a new earth*.

We are to be light, holding forth the word of life to those that are in our paths. We are to provide the good news of Christ so that all who will believe the gospel of Christ will be joined to His family.

His Church in the Wilderness
We are His Church, living in the wilderness provided for our first parents when they had to leave the Garden of Eden. Their *rejection* of God's laws for His creation was the reason for their *ejection.* Every generation since the beginning has had to live and work *under the control of the evil one.*

In God's power, we live in the middle—between God and Satan, between good and evil—a constant threat to Satan and his kingdom.

"But and if ye suffer for **righteous**ness' sake, happy are ye: and be not afraid of their terror, neither be troubled." 1 Peter 3:14

Yet, if we suffer for Christ, we endure, growing closer to Him, knowing more of the joy and fullness of His Spirit—thriving as He brings forth His fruit in us.

> "The righteous shall flourish like the palm tree:
> he shall grow like a cedar in Lebanon."
> Psalm 92:12

> "He that trusteth in his riches shall fall;
> but the righteous shall flourish as a branch."
> Proverbs 11:28

The Holy Spirit is the inspiration for the writing of God's Word and the presence and power in His Word for our defense against the evil one. The power of the Holy Spirit in us uses the sword of the Spirit—His Holy Word—to bring us from striving to surviving and victoriously thriving in Satan's hostile territory. We do well to meditate on God's Word to know ourselves and our enemy.

In the next chapter, we will share this storehouse of His Word concerning the difference in God's people and the world. We will see from these verses who are the righteous and ungodly; those of light and those of darkness, those of truth and deceit, those of life and death, of peace and oppression, of the Spirit and flesh.

It is by the power of His Spirit and His Word that brick and mortar walls fall down as He leads us on victoriously, joyfully, and fruitfully.

Dear Father in heaven, you continue to teach us and lead us onward in the power of the cross. Let your Spirit and Your Word do their work in the hearts and lives of your children. Bring those who are striving to the reality of surviving—and those who are surviving to **thriving***. In Jesus' name, I pray. Amen.*

30

Thriving in Enemy Territory

In this chapter, we will look closely at the lives of the children of God compared to the children of the world. Meditation and memorization of His promises are part of our strategy against Satan and his forces—our means of thriving in this world.

We must study the following verses and passages of Scripture as part of the soldier's manual if we are to survive and thrive in this world. This is a loaded chapter, more than I usually do with references, but needful for further study.

Armed

We must be armed to the teeth and transformed by *the renewing of our minds* with His Word—able to speak to the circumstances in our lives, else we will remain captive and be overcome. These references should give us encouragement and defense against our enemy at every turn and enable us to lead others to safety in our Lord Jesus Christ.

In His Word, God makes a difference in the *righteous* and the *ungodly.* There is **safety, strength, gladness and rejoicing and fruitfulness** in His kingdom. Added links are in parentheses.

> "Discern between the righteous and the wicked, between him that serveth God and him that serveth him not."
> Malachi 3:18

We see the destruction in Noah's day as a condemnation of the world.

> "By faith Noah, being warned of God of things not seen as yet, moved with fear, prepared an ark to the saving of his house; **by the which he condemned the world**, and became heir of the **righteous**ness which is by faith." Hebrews 11:7

In **Psalm 98:2** "The Lord made known his righteousness in the sight of the heathen."

In **Psalm 7:9** the wickedness of the wicked come to an end; but the just are established:"

"The arms of the wicked shall be broken: but the Lord upholdeth the righteous." **Psalm 37:17; (Psalm 75:10)**

> "For the eyes of the Lord are over the righteous, and his ears are open unto their prayers: but the face of the Lord is against them that do evil." 1 Peter 3:12

"The wicked are overthrown, the righteous shall stand." **Proverbs 12:7 (Psalm 129:4**; **Isaiah 11:4**)

Isaiah 26:10 teaches us that even if favor is shown to the wicked, he will not learn righteousness. He will still deal unjustly and not behold the majesty of the Lord.

> "The wicked flee when no man pursueth: but the righteous are bold as a lion." Proverbs 28:1

> "**Righteous**ness exalteth a nation: but sin is a reproach to any people." Proverbs 14:34

Proverbs 21:26 "He coveteth greedily all the day long: but the **righteous** giveth and spareth not.

"The mouth of the righteous speaketh wisdom." Psalm 37:30; (Psalm 7:11; Psalm 11:5; Proverbs 15:6; Proverbs 28:1)

There is Safety in the Lord

> "My tongue also shall talk of thy **righteous**ness all the day long: for they are confounded, for they are brought unto shame, that seek my hurt." Psalm 71:24; **Psalm 55:22** Zephaniah 2:3

> "The name of the Lord is a strong tower: the **righteous** runneth into it, and is safe." Proverbs 18:10

> "No weapon that is formed against thee shall prosper; and every tongue that shall rise against thee in judgment thou shalt condemn. This is the heritage of the servants of the Lord, and their **righteous**ness is of me, saith the Lord." Isaiah 54:17

He is our strength

> "But the salvation of the **righteous** is of the Lord: he is their strength in the time of trouble." Psalm 37:39

> "Fear thou not; for I am with thee: be not dismayed; for I am thy God: I will strengthen thee; yea, I will help thee; yea, I will uphold thee with the right hand of my righteousness." Isaiah 41:10 Isaiah 45:24

"The upright shall dwell in His presence" Psalm 140:13 **"with gladness and rejoicing."**

"The voice of rejoicing and salvation is in the tabernacles of the **righteous**: the right hand of the Lord doeth valiantly." Psalm 118:15

"I will greatly rejoice in the Lord, my soul shall be joyful in my God; for he hath clothed me with the garments of salvation, he hath covered me with the robe of **righteous**ness, as a bridegroom decketh himself with ornaments, and as a bride adorneth herself with her jewels."

"When the **righteous** are in authority, the people rejoice: but when the wicked beareth rule, the people mourn." Proverbs 29:2 (Psalm 32:11; Psalm 64:10; Psalm 33:1)

The Righteous Bear Fruit

"The wicked desireth the net of evil men: but the root of the **righteous** yieldeth fruit." Proverbs 12:12 (Isaiah 61:3)

"To appoint unto them that mourn in Zion, to give unto them beauty for ashes, the oil of joy for mourning, the garment of praise for the spirit of heaviness; that they might be called trees of **righteous**ness, the planting of the Lord, that he might be glorified." Isaiah 61:3 (Isaiah 3:10)

"Now he that ministereth seed to the sower both minister bread for your food, and multiply your seed sown, and increase the fruits of your **righteous**ness;"
2 Corinthians 9:10

"Now no chastening for the present seemeth to be joyous, but grievous: nevertheless afterward it yieldeth the peaceable fruit of **righteous**ness unto them which are exercised thereby." Hebrews 12:11

Light and Darkness

In the process of the Israelite's deliverance, Moses speaks of the Egyptians having no light, "but all the children of Israel had light in their dwellings" (Exodus 10:23).

"Unto the upright there ariseth light in the darkness." Psalm 112:4

"Light and gladness for the upright in heart." Psalm 97:11

> "The light of the **righteous** rejoiceth: but the lamp of the wicked shall be put out. He will bring me forth to the light, and I shall behold his **righteous**ness." Proverbs 13:9

> "Then shall the **righteous** shine forth as the sun in the kingdom of their Father." Matthew 13:43

Jesus spoke of "His light to those who would believe in the light and be the children of light." John 12:36

The apostle Paul defines God's people as ***children of light***.

> "That ye may be **blameless and harmless**, the **sons of God**, without rebuke, in the midst of a **crooked and perverse nation**, among whom ye shine as ***lights in the world***;" Philippians 2:15

> "Ye are all the **children of light**, and the children of the day; we are not of the night nor of darkness." 1 Thessalonians 5:5

Paul spoke of believers being "unequally yoked together with unbelievers: for what communion hath light with darkness?" 2 Corinthians 6:14

Truth and Deceit

> "They seek me daily, and delight to know my ways: they ask of me the ordinances of justice; they take delight in approaching to God." Isaiah 58:2

> "The Lord liveth, in truth, in judgment, and in **righteous**ness;" Jeremiah 4:2"

> "His word is true from the beginning: and endureth for ever." Psalm 119:160

> "He shall judge the world with **righteous**ness, and the people with his truth." Psalm 96:13

We see in the following verses how truth and righteousness are a combination for those who belong to Him, "and they shall be my people, and I will be their God, in truth and in **righteous**ness." Zechariah 8:8

"He layeth up sound wisdom for the **righteous**:" Proverbs 2:7
"The uprightly speak the truth." Psalm 15:2

> "The heart of the **righteous** studieth to answer: but the mouth of the wicked poureth out evil things." Proverbs 15:2

> "He that speaketh truth sheweth forth **righteous**ness: but a false witness deceit." Proverbs 12:17

He speaks encouragement to His people who are reproached of men.

> "Hearken unto me, ye that know **righteous**ness, the people in whose heart is my law; fear ye not the reproach of men, neither be ye afraid of their revilings." Isaiah 51:7

> "Let the lying lips be put to silence; which speak grievous things proudly and contemptuously against the **righteous**." Psalm 31:18

> "(For the fruit of the Spirit is in all goodness and **righteous**ness and truth;)" Ephesians 5:9

> "Stand therefore, having your loins girt about with truth, and having on the breastplate of **righteous**ness;" Ephesians 6:14

> "Therefore it is no great thing if his ministers also be transformed as the ministers of **righteous**ness; whose end shall be according to their works." 2 Corinthians 11:15

Life and Death

> "He that followeth after **righteous**ness and mercy findeth life, **righteous**ness, and honour." Proverbs 21:21

> "The mouth of a **righteous** man is a well of life: but violence covereth the mouth of the wicked." Proverbs 10:11

> "The **righteous**ness of thy testimonies is everlasting: give me understanding, and I shall live." Psalm 119:144

> "The wicked watcheth the **righteous,** and seeketh to slay him." Psalm 37:32; and gather themselves together against the soul of the **righteous.**" Psalm 94:21

> "The labour of the **righteous** tendeth to life: the fruit of the wicked to sin." Proverbs 10:16

"The lips of the **righteous** feed many: but fools die for want of wisdom." Proverbs 10:21
(Proverbs 3:32; Proverbs 10:32; Proverbs 12:5;)

"in the day of wrath **righteous**ness delivereth from death." Proverbs 11:4

Proverbs 10:2 in the way of **righteous**ness is life: and no death (Proverbs 12:28)

> "As **righteous**ness tendeth to life: so he that pursueth evil pursueth it to his own death." Proverbs 11:19

> "And these shall go away into everlasting punishment: but the **righteous** into life eternal." Matthew 25:46

> "That as sin hath reigned unto death, even so might grace reign through **righteous**ness unto eternal life by Jesus Christ our Lord." Romans 5:21

> "Neither yield ye your members as instruments of unrighteousness unto sin: but yield yourselves unto God, as those that are alive from the dead, and your members as instruments of **righteous**ness unto God." Romans 6:13

(Psalm 37:29; Psalm 119:144; Proverbs 10:3; Proverbs 10:25; Proverbs 16:8; Proverbs 10:28; Isaiah 51:6)

Peace and Oppression

> "And the work of **righteousness** shall be **peace**; and the effect of **righteousness** quietness **and** assurance for ever." Isaiah 32:17

> "For the kingdom of God is not meat and drink; but righteousness, and peace, and joy in the Holy Ghost." Romans 14:17

"And the fruit of **righteousness** is sown in **peace** of them that make **peace**." James 3:18

"Great **peace** have they which love thy law: and nothing shall offend them." Psalm 119:165

"And I delivered you out of the hand of the Egyptians, and out of the hand of all that **oppress**ed you, and drove them out from before you, and gave you their land;" Judges 6:9

"For strangers are risen up against me, and **oppress**ors seek after my soul: they have not set God before them." Psalm 54:3

"In **righteousness** shalt thou be established: thou shalt be far from **oppression**; for thou shalt not fear: and from terror; for it shall not come near thee." Isaiah 54:14

"The Lord executeth righteousness and judgment" Psalm 103:6 and a refuge for the **oppressed**," Psalm 9:9

There is a connection between Isaiah's prophecy of Jesus being *oppressed* and *afflicted* for us and the fulfillment of His power in *healing all that were oppressed of the devil.*

"He was **oppress**ed, and he was afflicted, yet he opened not his mouth: he is brought as a lamb to the slaughter, and as a sheep before her shearers is dumb, so he openeth not his mouth." Isaiah 53:7

"How God anointed Jesus of Nazareth with the Holy Ghost and with power: who went about doing good, and **healing all that were oppressed of the devil**; for God was with him." Acts 10:38 (Deuteronomy 26:7; Isaiah 49:26)

Spirit and Flesh

We close this chapter with the most profound teaching of God's Word for His people. The Christian life is more than just physical. It is a supernatural life given by the power of His Holy Spirit. The righteousness of Christ is ours by His Spirit, drawing us to Him and His living in us.

The Spirit of Christ within us is our only true defense and our means of thriving. His Spirit teaches us His Word and arms us with ***divine power to destroy strongholds, casting down imaginations and whatever exalts itself against the knowledge of Him and brings our thoughts captive to Christ.*** 2 Corinthians 10:4-5

> "Jesus answered, Verily, verily, I say unto thee, Except a man be born of water and of the Spirit, he cannot enter into the kingdom of God.
> That which is born of the flesh is flesh; and that which is born of the Spirit is spirit." John 3:5-6

Paul teaches more about the power of the Holy Spirit in the believer than any other New Testament writer. Read and study Romans 8:1-16. If you are not already familiar with this passage, spend time with this one and Galatians 5. Below are verses from these chapters.

> "That the **righteous**ness of the law might be fulfilled in us, who walk not after the flesh, but after the Spirit." Romans 8:4

> "And if Christ be in you, the body is dead because of sin; but the Spirit is life because of **righteous**ness." Romans 8:10

> "For we through the Spirit wait for the hope of **righteous**ness by faith." Galatians 5:5

"But I say, walk by the Spirit, and you will not gratify the desires of the flesh. For the desires of the flesh are against the Spirit, and the desires of the Spirit are against the flesh, for these are opposed to each other, to keep you from doing the things you want to do." Galatians 5:16-17

Paul gives a list of the dearies of the flesh in Galatians 5:19-21 "they which do such things shall not inherit the kingdom of God."

"But the fruit of the Spirit is love, joy, peace, longsuffering, gentleness, goodness, faith, meekness, temperance:
And they that are Christ's have crucified the flesh with the affections and lusts." Galatians 5:22-24

"For as the earth bringeth forth her bud, and as the garden causeth the things that are sown in it to spring forth; so the Lord God will cause **righteous**ness and praise to spring forth before all the nations." Isaiah 61:11

"I have sworn by myself, the word is gone out of my mouth in **righteous**ness, and shall not return, That unto me every knee shall bow, every tongue shall swear." Isaiah 45:23

Gracious Father in heaven, your Word is precious and powerful. By it, you created all things and by the Word of your power, you maintain. You birth your own children by it, fill us with the life that is in it, and you speak it through us for our defense and joy. We are not worthy, but we praise you for your written word; and more than this, for your Living Word—our Lord Jesus Christ. In His **name**, *we thank you and desire your continued Spirit leading us onward. In Jesus' name, I pray. Amen.*

31

Arrows in the Hands of a Mighty King

As I wrote this chapter, it was with a sense that I had not done justice to the truth and power of God's Word. I could not do anymore; but remembering Andrew Murray's words in the Foreword of his book *Waiting on God*, I quote these words, "I send these out with the prayer that He who uses the feeble may give a blessing with them."

Impressions from Other Authors

In three previous chapters, there have been references to books by authors I read years ago. Each one left an impression and from these, I have offered a challenge for us as God's children to go beyond what they wrote to search further into His Word.

God was speaking through them to be a witness of His kingdom and His salvation through Christ, His Son. They are dead and though they still speak through their books, God is still speaking through all His children today. We have nothing new since He spoke through His Son but we are called to be witnesses of what He reveals in His Word to each of us.

No person has all revelation but we each bring something to the feet of our Master for His anointing. It is the same faith, same Lord, same Father, same Spirit, and the same baptism through the person and work of Jesus Christ. But we never stop learning or growing.

We continue to search His Word, to pray for more than the average knowledge of our Lord—with which some are satisfied.

The title for this final chapter is based on two different ideas—the first is explained as we take a statement from a sermon and the second from the texts of Psalm 127:4 and Isaiah 49:2.

The Sermon
By reference to this sermon, we want to see the degrees from which, and to which, God calls us as His children.

On July 8, 1741, Jonathan Edwards delivered this sermon in Enfield, Connecticut. <u>Sinners in the Hands of an Angry God</u> is perhaps the most well-known and most heart-moving of sermons ever preached in America. (Instead of listening to an audio, please read it. Edwards was not an eloquent speaker but known for speaking word-for-word from his written documents.)

Let us consider these select words from His text.

> "The bow of God's wrath is bent, and the arrow made ready on the string, and justice bends the arrow at your heart, and strains the bow, and it is nothing but the mere pleasure of God, and that of an angry God, without any promise or obligation at all, that keeps the arrow one moment from being made drunk with your blood. Thus all you that never passed under a great change of heart, by the mighty power of the Spirit of God upon your souls; all you that were never born again, and made new creatures, and raised from being dead in sin, to a state of new, and before altogether unexperienced light and life, are in the hands of an angry God. However you may have reformed your life in many things, and may have had religious affections, and may keep up a form of religion in your families and closets, and in the

house of God, it is nothing but his mere pleasure that keeps you from being this moment swallowed up in everlasting destruction."₄

Our thoughts from this part of the sermon are focused on God's bow and arrow ready for his enemies. We find in the Old Testament such references:

In response to the rebellion of His people, Moses records the words of the Lord.

> "And he said, I will hide my face from them, I will see what their end shall be: for they are a very froward generation, children in whom is no faith. I will heap mischiefs upon them; I will spend mine **arrows** upon them."
> Deuteronomy 32:21-23

And upon His enemies are these words from the Psalmist.

> "Thine **arrows** are sharp in the heart of the king's enemies; whereby the people fall under thee." Psalm 45:5

At the end of his sermon, Edwards spoke the following words during which many were wailing and crying out for salvation.

> "And now you have an extraordinary opportunity, a day wherein Christ has thrown the door of mercy wide open and stands in calling and crying with a loud voice to poor sinners; a day wherein many are flocking to him and pressing into the kingdom of God."

In every generation, upon hearing the gospel, we, as His people, have conviction by the power of His Holy Spirit that brings us to repentance and faith.

₄ Sermon preached on July 8, 1741 at Enfield (blueletterbible.org)

I like to say that His arrows pierce our hearts and make us tremble at His Word so that we fall prostrate at His feet in need of a Savior.

He knows how to stop us in our tracks and turn us to Himself. He has the power to make His enemies not only His footstool but to make them His servants.

> **"Thy people shall be willing in the day of thy power."**
> Psalm 110:3

We see the promises of God's deliverance recorded in the Psalms and the Prophets.

> "The burden of the word of the Lord in the land of Hadrach, and Damascus shall be the rest thereof: **when the eyes of man, as of all the tribes of Israel, shall be toward the Lord.** And the Lord shall be seen over them, and his **arrow** shall go forth as the lightning: and the Lord God shall blow the trumpet, and shall go with whirlwinds of the south." Zechariah 9:1, 14 (See Zechariah 9 for the full impact of this promise of deliverance.)

God, the Father of our Lord Jesus Christ, Creator of the universe, has turned us from His wrath by sending us a King—the King of kings—to capture our hearts and turn us to Him. We are no longer His enemies but servants of the Most High God. He has made us His children and heirs to His kingdom.

He defends us and makes us His arrows even as we thrive in enemy territory. We are His quiver—His arrows against His and our enemies.

> "As **arrow**s are in the hand of a mighty man; so are children of the youth. Happy is the man that hath his **quiver** full of them: they shall not be ashamed, but they shall speak with the enemies in the gate." Psalm 127:4-5

Arrows in the Hands of a Mighty King 181

Such is our Father in heaven whose family on earth lives in defense of His kingdom.

> "And he hath made my mouth like a sharp sword; in the shadow of his hand hath he hid me, and made me a polished shaft; in his quiver hath he hid me," Isaiah 49:2

The Process by Which He Establishes His Army
Through His Word, He reveals Himself and births us into His kingdom, making us soldiers of the cross of Christ, His Son—the Mighty King who rules His kingdom. His Word is our manual for training.

His Holy Spirit continues to lead us to know our Master and King, to hear His voice, see Him, fear Him, love Him, obey Him, worship and serve Him, praise Him and pray to Him, to proclaim the name of Jesus Christ in power and to live for Him.

Our Response to His Mercy
By His mercy and by His covenant with us, He calls us to offer ourselves as living sacrifices—no longer conformed to this world, its god and its standards, but transformed by the renewing of our minds by His own Word and Spirit (Romans 12:1-2).

We survive victoriously and thrive in this wilderness so that the enemy knows who and where we are—as we live without fear of our enemies and always ready to ***defend the faith*** He alone gives (Jude).

He uses us to make known His name, His kingdom, and His will to others who will follow in His train.

As arrows designed for His purpose in the hands of our Mighty King, His power is wielded in us wherever and whenever He chooses.

Together, the following topics form the shape of an arrow. Starting with KNOW, we continue to HEAR, SEE, FEAR, and

LOVE to the point—OBEY—and through SERVE, WORSHIP, PRAISE, AND PRAY, we come to the point PROCLAIM.

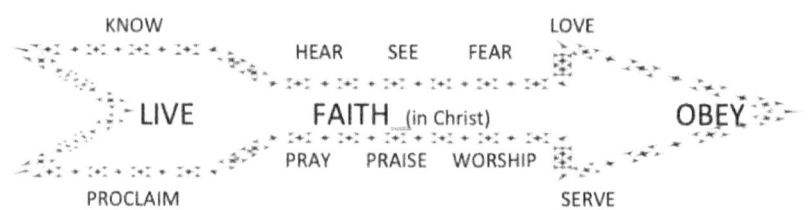

Living by Faith in Christ is the shaft that the King uses to drive the arrow forward in our obedience to hit the mark.

We will look at references to Know, Hear, See, Fear, Love, and Obey. In the arrow's underpart, we will look at references to Serve, Worship, Praise, Pray, Proclaim His Name and Live by faith in Him.

Rather than my commenting on these references, it would be good for us to meditate on each of these (there are actually many more than we have used). We need to establish time for one of these each day to build our repertoire of His manual.

KNOW

> "And Jesus came and spoke unto them, saying,
> All power is given unto me
> in heaven and in earth."
> Matthew 28:18

"All things are delivered to me of my Father: and no man **know**eth who the Son is, but the Father; and who the Father is, but the Son, and he to whom the Son will reveal him." Luke 10:22

"According as his divine power hath given unto us all things that pertain unto life and godliness, through the **know**ledge of him that hath called us to glory and virtue:" 2 Peter 1:3

**"Be still, and know that I am God:
I will be exalted among the heathen,
I will be exalted in the earth."** Psalm 46:10

"Nevertheless he saved them for his name's sake, that he might make his mighty power to be **know**n." Psalm 106:8

"And I will give them an heart to **know** me, that I am the Lord: and they shall be my people, and I will be their God: for they shall return unto me with their whole heart." Jeremiah 24:7

"But let him that glorieth glory in this, that he understandeth and **know**eth me, that I am the Lord which exercise lovingkindness, judgment, and righteousness, in the earth: for in these things I delight, saith the Lord." Jeremiah 9:24

"And they shall teach no more every man his neighbour, and every man his brother, saying, **Know** the Lord: for they shall all **know** me, from the least of them unto the greatest of them, saith the Lord: for I will forgive their iniquity, and I will remember their sin no more." Jeremiah 31:34

Known by His Shepherds and His Sheep

"And I will give you pastors according to mine heart, which shall feed you with **know**ledge and understanding." Jeremiah 3:15

"**Know** ye that the Lord he is God: it is he that hath made us, and not we ourselves; we are his people, and the sheep of his pasture." Psalm 100:3

"And when he putteth forth his own sheep, he goeth before them, and the sheep follow him: for they **know** his voice." John 10:4

"I am the good shepherd, and **know** my sheep, and am **know**n of mine." John 10:14

"He answered and said unto them, Because it is given unto you to **know** the mysteries of the kingdom of heaven, but to them it is not given." Matthew 13:11

"That I may **know** him, and the power of his resurrection, and the fellowship of his sufferings, being made conformable unto his death;" Philippians 3:10

"the excellency of the **know**ledge of Christ Jesus my Lord:" Philippians 3:8; Deuteronomy 4:39; Nahum 1:7; Psalm 67:2

HEAR

"And they **hear**d the **voice** of the Lord God walking in the garden in the cool of the day: and Adam and **his** wife hid themselves from the presence of the Lord God amongst the trees of the garden." Genesis 3:8

"The Lord God hath given me the tongue of the learned, that I should **know** how to speak a word in season to him that is weary: he wakeneth morning by morning, he wakeneth mine ear to hear as the learned." Isaiah 50:4

"While it is said, Today if ye will **hear his voice**, harden not your **hear**ts, as in the provocation." Hebrews 3:15

"When thou shalt **hear**ken to the **voice** of the Lord thy God, to keep all **his** commandments which I command thee this day, to do that which is right in the eyes of the Lord thy God." Deuteronomy 13:18

"He that hath ears to **hear**, let him **hear**." Matthew 11:15

"For verily I say unto you, That many prophets and righteous men have desired to see those things which ye see, and have not seen them; and to **hear** those things which ye **hear**, and have not **heard** them." Matthew 13:17

"While he yet spake, behold, a bright cloud overshadowed them: and behold a voice out of the cloud, which said, This is my beloved Son, in whom I am well pleased; **hear** ye him." Matthew 17:5

"And he said unto them, Take heed what ye **hear**: with what measure ye mete, it shall be measured to you: and unto you that **hear** shall more be given." Mark 4:24

"But I say unto you which **hear**, Love your enemies, do good to them which hate you," Luke 6:27

"Take heed therefore how ye **hear**: for whosoever hath, to him shall be given; and whosoever hath not, from him shall be taken even that which he seemeth to have." Luke 8:18

"And he answered and said unto them, My mother and my brethren are these which **hear** the word of God, and do it." Luke 8:21

"But he said, Yea rather, blessed are they that **hear** the word of God, and keep it." Luke 11:28

> "My sheep **hear** my voice, and I **know** them,
> and they follow me:"
> John 10:27

"Pilate therefore said unto him, Art thou a king then? Jesus answered, Thou sayest that I am a king. To this end was I born, and for this cause came I into the world, that I should bear witness unto the truth. Every one that is of the truth **hear**eth my voice." John 18:37

"And said unto the woman, Now we believe, not because of thy saying: for we have **heard** him ourselves, and **know** that this is indeed the Christ, the Saviour of the world." John 4:42

SEE

"And he said, The God of our fathers hath chosen thee, that thou shouldest know his will, and see that Just One, and shouldest hear the voice of his mouth." Acts 22:14

"The **eyes** of your understanding being enlightened; that ye may **know** what is the hope of his calling, and what the riches of the glory of his inheritance in the saints," Ephesians 1:18

"But blessed are your eyes, for they **see:** and your ears, for they **hear**. For verily I say unto you, That many prophets and righteous men have desired to **see** those things which ye **see**, and have not seen them; and to **hear** those things which ye **hear**, and have not **hear**d them." Matthew 13:16-17

FEAR

"The **fear** of the Lord is the beginning of wisdom: and the **know**ledge of the holy is understanding." Proverbs 9:10

"Hearken unto me, ye that **know** righteousness, the people in whose heart is my law; **fear** ye not the reproach of men, neither be ye afraid of their revilings." Isaiah 51:7

"I **know** that, whatsoever God doeth, It shall be for ever: nothing can be put to it, nor any thing taken from it: and God doeth it, that men should **fear** before him." Ecclesiastes 3:14

"And the spirit of the Lord shall rest upon him, the spirit of wisdom and understanding, the spirit of counsel and might, the spirit of **know**ledge and of the **fear** of the Lord;" Isaiah 11:2

"And this was **know**n to all the Jews and Greeks also dwelling at Ephesus; and **fear** fell on them all, and the name of the Lord Jesus was magnified." Acts 19:17

LOVE

"Because he hath set his love upon me, therefore will I deliver him: I will set him on high, because he hath known my name." Psalm 91:14

"Jesus said unto him, Thou shalt **love** the Lord thy God with all thy **hear**t, and with all thy soul, and with all thy mind." Matthew 22:37

"But whoso keepeth his word, in him verily is the **love** of God perfected: hereby **know** we that we are in him." 1 John 2:5

> "**Herein is love, not that we loved God,
> but that he loved us, and sent his Son
> to be the propitiation for our sins.**"
> 1 John 4:10

"And we have **know**n and believed the **love** that God hath to us. God is **love**; and he that dwelleth in **love** dwelleth in God, and God in him." 1 John 4:16

"And this I pray, that your **love** may abound yet more and more in **know**ledge and in all judgment;" Philippians 1:9

"By this shall all men **know** that ye are my disciples, if ye have **love** one to another." John 13:35

"We **know** that we have passed from death unto life, because we **love** the brethren. He that loveth not his brother abideth in death." 1 John 3:14

"Hereby perceive we the love of God, because he laid down his life for us: and we ought to lay down our lives for the brethren." 1 John 3:16

"Beloved, let us l**ove one** another: for l**ove** is of God; and every one that **loveth** is born of God, and **know**eth God." 1 John 4:7

In the next and last chapter, we will look at the power of living by faith in Jesus Christ that brings about obedience to our Master and King. We will see the effects of living in obedience as we serve, worship, praise, pray and proclaim the name of Christ.

Gracious Father in heaven, we praise you for the power of your Holy Spirit to bring us captive to Christ, that we may be free to serve and worship you without fear of our enemies. Shape us as your arrows as you are conforming us to the image of your dear Son. In Jesus' precious name, I pray, Amen.

32

The Shaft of Faith

This has been a strenuous but joyful undertaking, as I have been mining God's Word to find the treasures He has hidden there for us. As we saw in the design of His arrows, faith is the shaft, the core of our relationship to Him as He makes us His arrows, revealing through us His power here on earth.

As with all things pertaining to His kingdom and rule in heaven and earth, faith comes from Him. Just as He is love and we love because He first loved us, so He is faithful to us, faithful before we ever knew Him, and by His grace, to bring us to faith in His Son, Jesus Christ in His timing, and to keep us in Him by the power of His Holy Spirit.

God's Faithfulness

"O love the Lord, all ye his saints: for the Lord preserveth the **faith**ful, and plentifully rewardeth the proud doer." Psalm 31:23

"For I have said, Mercy shall be built up for ever: thy **faith**fulness shalt thou establish in the very heavens." Psalm 89:2

"Thy **faith**fulness is unto all generations: thou hast established the earth, and it abideth." Psalm 119:90

"But my **faith**fulness and my mercy shall be with him: and in my name shall his horn be exalted." Psalm 89:24

"But the Lord is **faith**ful, who shall stablish you, and keep you from evil." 2 Thessalonians 3:3

"I will even betroth thee unto me in **faith**fulness: and thou shalt know the Lord." Hosea 2:20

> **"God is faithful,
> by whom ye were called unto the fellowship
> of his Son Jesus Christ our Lord."**
> 1 Corinthians 1:9

"There hath no temptation taken you but such as is common to man: but God is **faith**ful, who will not suffer you to be tempted above that ye are able; but will with the temptation also make a way to escape, that ye may be able to bear it." 1 Corinthians 10:13

"And they that **know** thy name will put their trust in thee: for thou, Lord, hast not forsaken them that seek thee." Psalm 9:10

Faith of and in Jesus Christ

"To open their eyes, and to turn them from darkness to light, and from the power of Satan unto God, that they may receive forgiveness of sins, and inheritance among them which are sanctified by **faith** that is in me." Acts 26:18

"Even the righteousness of God which is by **faith** of Jesus Christ unto all and upon all them that believe: for there is no difference:" Romans 3:22

"By whom also we have access by **faith** into this grace wherein we stand, and rejoice in hope of the glory of God." Romans 5:2

"I am crucified with Christ: nevertheless I live; yet not I, but Christ liveth in me: and the life which I now live in the flesh I live by the **faith** of the Son of God, who loved me, and gave himself for me.: Galatians 2:20

> "For ye are all the children of God
> by faith in Christ Jesus."
> Galatians 3;26

"For though I be absent in the flesh, yet am I with you in the spirit, joying and beholding your order, and the stedfastness of your **faith** in Christ." Colossians 2:5

"Rooted and built up in him, and stablished in the **faith**, as ye have been taught, abounding therein with thanksgiving." Colossians 2:7

"Buried with him in baptism, wherein also ye are risen with him through the **faith** of the operation of God, who hath raised him from the dead." Colossians 2:12

"Examine yourselves, whether ye be in the **faith**; prove your own selves. Know ye not your own selves, how that Jesus Christ is in you, except ye be reprobates?" 2 Corinthians 13:5

"Looking unto Jesus the author and finisher of our **faith**; who for the joy that was set before him endured the cross, despising the shame, and is set down at the right hand of the throne of God." Hebrews 12:2

Faith by the Word of God

> "So then faith cometh by hearing,
> and hearing by the word of God."
> Romans 10:17

"But what saith it? The word is nigh thee, even in thy mouth, and in thy heart: that is, the word of **faith**, which we preach." Romans 10:8

"And the scripture, foreseeing that God would justify the heathen through **faith**, preached before the gospel unto Abraham, saying, In thee shall all nations be blessed." Galatians 3:8

"If ye continue in the **faith** grounded and settled, and be not moved away from the hope of the gospel, which ye have heard, and which was preached to every creature which is under heaven; whereof I Paul am made a minister;" Colossians 1:23

"Holding fast the **faith**ful word as he hath been taught, that he may be able by sound doctrine both to exhort and to convince the gainsayers." Titus 1:9

Faith by the Power of God

"That your **faith** should not stand in the wisdom of men, but in the power of God." 1 Corinthians 2:5

"Wherefore also we pray always for you, that our God would count you worthy of this calling, and fulfil all the good pleasure of his goodness, and the work of **faith** with power:"
2 Thessalonians 1:11

> **"Who are kept by the power of God
> through faith unto salvation
> ready to be revealed in the last time."**
> 1 Peter 1:5

Faith by Grace

"Therefore it is of **faith**, that it might be by grace; to the end the promise might be sure to all the seed; not to that only which is of the law, but to that also which is of the **faith** of Abraham; who is the father of us all," Romans 4:16

"For by grace are ye saved through faith; and that not of yourselves: it is the gift of God:"
Ephesians 2:8

Faith and Righteousness

"And be found in him, not having mine own righteousness, which is of the law, but that which is through the **faith** of Christ, the righteousness which is of God by **faith**:" Philippians 3:9

"Simon Peter, a servant and an apostle of Jesus Christ, to them that have obtained like precious **faith** with us through the righteousness of God and our Saviour Jesus Christ:" 2 Peter 1:1

Faith and Justification

"Therefore we conclude that a man is justified by **faith** without the deeds of the law." Romans 3:28

"Therefore being justified by faith, we have peace with God through our Lord Jesus Christ:"
Romans 5:1

"But to him that worketh not, but believeth on him that justifieth the ungodly, his **faith** is counted for righteousness." Romans 4:5

"But that no man is justified by the law in the sight of God, it is evident: for, The just shall live by **faith**." Galatians 3:11

"Knowing that a man is not justified by the works of the law, but by the **faith** of Jesus Christ, even we have believed in Jesus Christ, that we might be justified by the **faith** of Christ, and not by the works of the law: for by the works of the law shall no flesh be justified." Galatians 2:16

The Measure of Faith

"He that is **faith**ful in that which is least is **faith**ful also in much: and he that is unjust in the least is unjust also in much." Luke 16:10

"For I say, through the grace given unto me, to every man that is among you, not to think of himself more highly than he ought to think; but to think soberly, according as God hath dealt to every man the measure of **faith**." Romans 12:3

Faith and the Holy Spirit

"And the saying pleased the whole multitude: and they chose Stephen, a man full of **faith** and of the Holy Ghost, and Philip, and Prochorus, and Nicanor, and Timon, and Parmenas, and Nicolas a proselyte of Antioch:" Acts 6:5

> **"But the fruit of the Spirit is love, joy, peace, longsuffering, gentleness, goodness, faith,"**
> Galatians 5:22

Increase of Faith

"Not boasting of things without our measure, that is, of other men's labours; but having hope, when your **faith** is increased, that we shall be enlarged by you according to our rule abundantly," 2 Corinthians 10:15

"And the apostles said unto the Lord,
Increase our faith."
Luke 17:5

"We are bound to thank God always for you, brethren, as it is meet, because that your **faith** groweth exceedingly, and the charity of every one of you all toward each other aboundeth;" 2 Thessalonians 1:3

The Household of Faith

"As we have therefore opportunity, let us do good unto all men, especially unto them who are of the household of **faith**." Galatians 6:10

"Only let your conversation be as it becometh the gospel of Christ: that whether I come and see you, or else be absent, I may hear of your affairs, that ye stand fast in one spirit, with one mind striving together for the **faith** of the gospel;" Philippians 1:27

"Neither give heed to fables and endless genealogies, which minister questions, rather than godly edifying which is in **faith**: so do." 1 Timothy 1:4

"Paul, a servant of God, and an apostle of Jesus Christ, according to the **faith** of God's elect, and the acknowledging of the truth which is after godliness;" Titus 1:1

Faith and Love

"For in Jesus Christ neither circumcision availeth any thing, nor uncircumcision; but **faith** which worketh by love." Galatians 5:6

"But let us, who are of the day, be sober, putting on the breastplate of **faith** and love; and for an helmet, the hope of salvation."
1 Thessalonians 5:8

"Hearing of thy love and **faith**, which thou hast toward the Lord Jesus, and toward all saints;" Phiemon 1:5

Faith and Trials

"Confirming the souls of the disciples, and exhorting them to continue in the faith, and that we must through much tribulation enter into the kingdom of God." Acts 14:22"

"That the trial of your **faith**, being much more precious than of gold that perisheth, though it be tried with fire, might be found unto praise and honour and glory at the appearing of Jesus Christ:" 1 Peter 1:7

> "For whatsoever is born of God
> overcometh the world:
> and this is the victory that overcometh the world,
> even our faith."
> 1 John 5:4

Strength and Boldness of Faith

"In whom we have boldness and access with confidence by the **faith** of him." Ephesians 3;12

"He staggered not at the promise of God through unbelief; but was strong in **faith**, giving glory to God;" Romans 4:20

"Watch ye, stand fast in the **faith**, quit you like men, be strong. 1 Corinthians 16:13

"Above all, taking the shield of **faith**, wherewith ye shall be able to quench all the fiery darts of the wicked." Ephesians 6:16

"Whom resist stedfast in the **faith**, knowing that the same afflictions are accomplished in your brethren that are in the world." 1 Peter 5:9

> **"We should earnestly contend for the faith which was once delivered unto the saints."**
> Jude 3

Faith and Patience

"So that we ourselves glory in you in the churches of God for your patience and **faith** in all your persecutions and tribulations that ye endure:" 2 Thessalonians 1:4

"Remembering without ceasing your work of **faith**, and labour of love, and patience of hope in our Lord Jesus Christ, in the sight of God and our Father;" 1 Thessalonians 1:3

"That ye be not slothful, but followers of them who through **faith** and patience inherit the promises." Hebrews 6:12

> **"Knowing this, that the trying of your faith worketh patience."**
> James 1:3

"He that leadeth into captivity shall go into captivity: he that killeth with the sword must be killed with the sword. Here is the patience and the **faith** of the saints." Revelation 13:10

"Here is the patience of the saints: here are they that keep the commandments of God, and the **faith** of Jesus." Revelation 14:12

"These shall make war with the Lamb, and the Lamb shall overcome them: for he is Lord of lords, and King of kings: and they that are with him are called, and chosen, and **faith**ful." Revelation 17:14

Meditation on these truths will strengthen and increase our faith for the work of His kingdom—at the same time increasing our joy and fellowship with Him.

Dear Father, what an undertaking you give us for the proving of our faith. And what a blessing to dig deeper into your Word to find the precious nuggets you have hidden there for us. Fill our hearts with faith and love for you as you are always faithful in your promises for us. In Jesus' name, I pray. Amen

33

Living by Faith

(For we walk by faith, not by sight:)
2 Corinthians 5:7

In this chapter, we will look at how God has designed the underside of His arrows. Again, we see Faith in Christ as the center—the heart of every Christian. We begin our relationship with Him as He has planned—for us to know Him, hear, see, fear, and love Him. This brings us to the point of obedience. Living by faith, we obey, serve, worship, praise, pray, and proclaim His kingdom in power.

Some of these chapters have been longer than we would have desired but necessary for this book. There is much here of God's Word that you may only scan but hopefully, a quote will speak to your heart and you can keep them all for future reference.

The Point and Result of Faith

"And the law is not of **faith**: but, The man that doeth them shall live in them." Galatians 3:12

"Now **faith** is the substance of things hoped for, the evidence of things not seen." Hebrews 11:1

"But without **faith** it is impossible to please him: for he that cometh to God must believe that he is, and that he is a rewarder of them that diligently seek him." Hebrews 11:6

OBEY

"And in thy seed shall all the nations of the earth be blessed; because thou hast **obey**ed my voice." Genesis 22:18

"And the kingdom and dominion, and the greatness of the kingdom under the whole heaven, shall be given to the people of the saints of the most High, whose kingdom is an everlasting kingdom, and all dominions shall serve and **obey** him." Daniel 7:27

"Then Peter and the other apostles answered and said, We ought to **obey** God rather than men." Acts 5:29

"And the word of God increased; and the number of the disciples multiplied in Jerusalem greatly; and a great company of the priests were obedient to the **faith**." Acts 6:7

In four verses, Paul speaks in his letter to the Romans of *obedience to and of faith.*

> **"By whom we have received grace and apostleship, for obedience to the faith among all nations, for his name:"**
> Romans 1:5

"**Know** ye not, that to whom ye yield yourselves servants to obey, his servants ye are to whom ye obey; whether of sin unto death, or of **obedience** unto righteousness?
But God be thanked, that ye were the servants of sin, but ye have **obey**ed from the heart that form of doctrine which was delivered you." Romans 6:16-17

"But now is made manifest, and by the scriptures of the prophets, according to the commandment of the everlasting God, made **know**n to all nations for the **obedience** of faith:" Romans 16:26

"Casting down imaginations, and every high thing that exalteth itself against the **know**ledge of God, and bringing into captivity every thought to the **obedience** of Christ;" 2 Corinthians 10:5 Exodus 19:5; Zechariah 6:15; Acts 5:32; 1 Peter 1:22

SERVE

"**Serve** the Lord with fear, and rejoice with trembling." Psalm 2:11

> "**Serve the Lord with gladness:
> come before his presence with singing.**"
> Psalm 100:2

"Mine eyes shall be upon the **faith**ful of the land, that they may dwell with me: he that walketh in a perfect way, he shall **serve** me." Psalm 101:6

"That he would grant unto us, that we being delivered out of the hand of our enemies might **serve** him without fear," Luke 1:74

"If any man **serve** me, let him follow me; and where I am, there shall also my servant be: if any man **serve** me, him will my Father honour." John 12:2

"But now we are delivered from the law, that being dead wherein we were held; that we should **serve** in newness of spirit, and not in the oldness of the letter." Romans 7:6

"For he that in these things **serve**th Christ is acceptable to God, and approved of men." Romans 14:18

"For, brethren, ye have been called unto liberty; only use not liberty for an occasion to the flesh, but by love **serve** one another." Galatians 5:13

"Knowing that of the Lord ye shall receive the reward of the inheritance: for ye **serve** the Lord Christ." Colossians 3:24

"For they themselves shew of us what manner of entering in we had unto you, and how ye turned to God from idols to **serve** the living and true God." 1 Thessalonians 1:9

"How much more shall the blood of Christ, who through the eternal Spirit offered himself without spot to God, purge your conscience from dead works to **serve** the living God?" Hebrews 9:14

"Wherefore we receiving a kingdom which cannot be moved, let us have grace, whereby we may **serve** God acceptably with reverence and godly fear:" Hebrews 12:28

"And there shall be no more curse: but the throne of God and of the Lamb shall be in it; and his servants shall **serve** him:" Revelation 22:3

WORSHIP

"Give unto the Lord the glory due unto his name; **worship** the Lord in the beauty of holiness." Psalm 29:2

"So shall the king greatly desire thy beauty: for he is thy Lord; and **worship** thou him." Psalm 45:11

"I will **worship** toward thy holy temple, and praise thy name for thy lovingkindness and for thy truth: for thou hast magnified thy word above all thy name." Psalm 138:2

> **"God is a Spirit:**
> **and they that worship him must worship him**
> **in spirit and in truth."**
> John 4:24

"Now we know that God heareth not sinners: but if any man be a **worship**per of God, and doeth his will, him he heareth." John 9:31

"Who shall not fear thee, O Lord, and glorify thy name? for thou only art holy: for all nations shall come and **worship** before thee; for thy judgments are made manifest." Revelation 15:4

PRAISE

"Now therefore, our God, we thank thee, and **praise** thy glorious name." 1 Chronicles 29:13

"While I **live** will I **praise** the Lord: I will sing praises unto my God while I have any being." Psalm 146:2

"I will **praise** the Lord according to his righteousness: and will sing **praise** to the name of the Lord most high." Psalm 7:17

"Therefore will I give thanks unto thee, O Lord, among the heathen, and sing **praise**s unto thy name." Psalm 18:49

> **"Be thou exalted, Lord, in thine own strength:**
> **so will we sing and praise thy power."**
> Psalm 21:1

"But thou art holy, O thou that inhabitest the **praise**s of Israel." Psalm 22:3

"The Lord is my strength and my shield; my heart trusted in him, and I am helped: therefore my heart greatly rejoiceth; and with my song will I **praise** him." Psalm 28:7

"I will bless the Lord at all times: his **praise** shall continually be in my mouth." Psalm 34:1

"And he hath put a new song in my mouth, even **praise** unto our God: many shall see it, and fear, and shall trust in the Lord." Psalm 40:3

"Why art thou cast down, O my soul? and why art thou disquieted in me? hope thou in God: for I shall yet **praise** him for the help of his countenance." Psalm 42:5

"Whoso offereth **praise** glorifieth me: and to him that ordereth his conversation aright will I shew the salvation of God." Psalm 50:23

"O Lord, open thou my lips; and my mouth shall shew forth thy **praise**." Psalm 51:15

"In God will I **praise** his word: in the Lord will I **praise** his word." Psalm 56:10

"My heart is fixed, O God, my heart is fixed: I will sing and give **praise**." Psalm 57:7

"Sing forth the honour of his name: make him **praise** glorious." Psalm 66:2

"But I will hope continually, and will yet **praise** thee more and more." Psalm 71:14

"**Praise** ye the Lord. O give thanks unto the Lord; for he is good: for his mercy endureth for ever." Psalm 106:1

"Oh that men would **praise** the Lord for his goodness, and for his wonderful works to the children of men!" Psalm 107:8

"From the rising of the sun unto the going down of the same the Lord's name is to be **praise**d." Psalm 113:3

"He hath not dealt so with any nation: and as for his judgments, they have not known them. **Praise** ye the Lord." Psalm 147:20

"Let the high **praise**s of God be in their mouth, and a two-edged sword in their hand;" Psalm 149:6

"O Lord, thou art my God; I will exalt thee, I will praise thy name; for thou hast done wonderful things; thy counsels of old are **faith**fulness and truth." Isaiah 25:1

> **"To the praise of the glory of his grace,**
> **wherein he hath made us**
> **accepted in the beloved."**
> Ephesians 1:6

"Being filled with the fruits of righteousness, which are by Jesus Christ, unto the glory and **praise** of God." Philippians 1:11

"By him therefore let us offer the sacrifice of **praise** to God continually, that is the fruit of our lips giving thanks to his name." Hebrews 13:15

"That the trial of your faith, being much more precious than of gold that perisheth, though it be tried with fire, might be found unto **praise** and honour and glory at the appearing of Jesus Christ:" 1 Peter 1:7

"But ye are a chosen generation, a royal priesthood, an holy nation, a peculiar people; that ye should shew forth the **praise**s of him who hath called you out of darkness into his marvellous light;" 1 Peter 2:9

PRAY

"And the people cried unto Moses; and when Moses **pray**ed unto the Lord, the fire was quenched." Numbers 11:2

"Now when Solomon had made an end of **pray**ing, the fire came down from heaven, and consumed the burnt offering and the sacrifices; and the glory of the Lord filled the house." 2 Chronicles 7:1

"If my people, which are called by my name, shall humble themselves, and **pray**, and seek my face, and turn from their wicked ways; then will I hear from heaven, and will forgive their sin, and will heal their land." 2 Chronicles 7:14

"But I say unto you, Love your enemies, bless them that curse you, do good to them that hate you, and **pray** for them which despitefully use you, and persecute you;" Matthew 5:44

"But thou, when thou **pray**est, enter into thy closet, and when thou hast shut thy door, **pray** to thy Father which is in secret; and thy Father which seeth in secret shall reward thee openly." Matthew 6:6

"**Pray** ye therefore the Lord of the harvest, that he will send forth labourers into his harvest." Matthew 9:38

"And all things, whatsoever ye shall ask in **pray**er, believing, ye shall receive." Matthew 21:22

"Watch and **pray**, that ye enter not into temptation: the spirit indeed is willing, but the flesh is weak." Matthew 26:41

"And in the morning, rising up a great while before day, he went out, and departed into a solitary place, and there **pray**ed." Mark 1:35

"And when ye stand **pray**ing, forgive, if ye have ought against any: that your Father also which is in heaven may forgive you your trespasses." Mark 11:25

"And he said unto them, When ye **pray**, say, Our Father which art in heaven, Hallowed be thy name. Thy kingdom come. Thy will be done, as in heaven, so in earth." Luke 11:2

"And he spake a parable unto them to this end, that men ought always to **pray**, and not to faint;" Luke 18:1

"Watch ye therefore, and **pray** always, that ye may be accounted worthy to escape all these things that shall come to pass, and to stand before the Son of man." Luke 21:36

"Now we know that God **hear**eth not sinners: but if any man be a worshipper of God, and doeth his will, him he **hear**eth." John 9:31

"Likewise the Spirit also helpeth our infirmities: for we know not what we should **pray** for as we ought: but the Spirit itself maketh intercession for us with groanings which cannot be uttered." Romans 8:26

"Rejoicing in hope; patient in tribulation; continuing instant in **pray**er;" Romans 12:12

"**Pray**ing always with all **pray**er and supplication in the Spirit, and watching thereunto with all perseverance and supplication for all saints;" Ephesians 6:18

"Be careful for nothing; but in every thing by **pray**er and supplication with thanksgiving let your requests be made known unto God." Philippians 4:6

"Pray without ceasing."
1 Thessalonians 5:17

"I exhort therefore, that, first of all, supplications, **pray**ers, intercessions, and giving of thanks, be made for all men;" 1 Timothy 2:1

"Is any among you afflicted? let him **pray**. Is any merry? let him sing psalms." James 5:13

"Confess your faults one to another, and **pray** one for another, that ye may be healed. The effectual fervent **pray**er of a righteous man availeth much." James 5:16

"And if we **know** that he hear us, whatsoever we ask, we **know** that we have the petitions that we desired of him." 1 John 5:15

"But ye, beloved, building up yourselves on your most holy faith, **pray**ing in the Holy Ghost," Jude 20

"And the smoke of the incense, which came with the **pray**ers of the saints, ascended up before God out of the angel's hand." Revelation 8:4

PROCLAIM

"And in very deed for this cause have I raised thee up, for to shew in thee my power; and that my name may be **declare**d throughout all the earth." Exodus 9:16

"And the Lord passed by before him, and **proclaim**ed, The Lord, The Lord God, merciful and gracious, longsuffering, and abundant in goodness and truth," Exodus 34:6

> **"Declare his glory among the heathen;
> his marvellous works among all nations."**
> 1 Chronicles 16:24

"They shall come, and shall **declare** his righteousness unto a people that shall be born, that he hath done this." Psalm 22:31

"Come and hear, all ye that fear God, and I will **declare** what he hath done for my soul." Psalm 66:16

"But it is good for me to draw near to God: I have put my trust in the Lord God, that I may **declare** all thy works." Psalm 73:28

"And men shall speak of the might of thy terrible acts: and I will **declare** thy greatness." Psalm 145:6

"A true **witness** delivereth souls: but a deceitful **witness** speaketh lies." Proverbs 14:25

"I have **declare**d, and have saved, and I have shewed, when there was no strange god among you: therefore ye are my witnesses, saith the Lord, that I am God." Isaiah 43:12

"Fear ye not, neither be afraid: have not I told thee from that time, and have declared it? ye are even my **witness**es. Is there a God beside me? yea, there is no God; I know not any." Isaiah 44:8

"Thou hast heard, see all this; and will not ye **declare** it? I have shewed thee new things from this time, even hidden things, and thou didst not know them." Isaiah 48:6

"Go ye forth of Babylon, flee ye from the Chaldeans, with a voice of singing **declare** ye, tell this, utter it even to the end of the earth; say ye, The Lord hath redeemed his servant Jacob." Isaiah 48:20

"The Spirit of the Lord God is upon me; because the Lord hath anointed me to preach good tidings unto the meek; he hath sent me to bind up the brokenhearted, to **proclaim** liberty to the captives, and the opening of the prison to them that are bound;" Isaiah 61:1

"The prophet that hath a dream, let him tell a dream; and he that hath my word, let him speak my word **faith**fully. What is the chaff to the wheat? saith the Lord." Jeremiah 23:28

"Hear the word of the Lord, O ye nations, and **declare** it in the isles afar off, and say, He that scattered Israel will gather him, and keep him, as a shepherd doth his flock." Jeremiah 31:10

"And this gospel of the kingdom shall be preached in all the world for a **witness** unto all nations; and then shall the end come." Matthew 24:14

"Therefore whatsoever ye have spoken in darkness shall be heard in the light; and that which ye have spoken in the ear in closets shall be **proclaim**ed upon the housetops." Luke 12:3

"He was not that Light, but was sent to bear **witness** of that Light." John 1:8

"But ye shall receive power, after that the Holy Ghost is come upon you: and ye shall be **witness**es unto me both in Jerusalem, and in all Judaea, and in Samaria, and unto the uttermost part of the earth." Acts 1:8

"And when they were come to Jerusalem, they were received of the church, and of the apostles and elders, and they **declare**d all things that God had done with them." Acts 15:4

"For I have not shunned to **declare** unto you all the counsel of God." Acts 20:27

> **"For thou shalt be his witness unto all men of what thou hast seen and heard."**
> Acts 22:15

"Moreover, brethren, I **declare** unto you the gospel which I preached unto you, which also ye have received, and wherein ye stand;" 1 Corinthians 15:1

"Now thanks be unto God, which always cause thus to triumph in Christ, and maketh manifest the savour of his **know**ledge by us in every place." 2 Corinthians 2:14

"And for me, that utterance may be given unto me, that I may open my mouth boldly, to make **known** the mystery of the gospel," Ephesians 6:19

"Fight the good fight of **faith**, lay hold on eternal life, whereunto thou art also called, and hast professed a good profession before many witnesses." 1 Timothy 6:12

"And the things that thou hast heard of me among many **witness**es, the same commit thou to faithful men, who shall be able to teach others also." 2 Timothy 2:2

"If any man speak, let him speak as the oracles of God; if any man minister, let him do it as of the ability which God giveth: that God in all things may be glorified through Jesus Christ, to whom be **praise** and dominion for ever and ever. Amen." 1 Peter 4:11

"That which we have seen and heard **declare** we unto you, that ye also may have fellowship with us: and truly our fellowship is with the Father, and with his Son Jesus Christ." 1 John 1:3

"This then is the message which we have heard of him, and **declare** unto you, that God is light, and in him is no darkness at all." 2 John 1:5

"If we receive the **witness** of men, the **witness** of God is greater: for this is the **witness** of God which he hath testified of his Son." 1 John 5:9

"He that believeth on the Son of God hath the **witness** in himself: he that believeth not God hath made him a liar; because he believeth not the record that God gave of his Son." 1 John 5:10

Dear Father, full of mercy and truth, thank you for saving us to be your own children. Fill us with your Spirit and increase our knowledge and faith in our Lord Jesus Christ. Let us hear, see, fear, and love you to the point of obeying your Holy Word. Instruct and equip us to serve you, worship, praise, pray, and proclaim your kingdom in power. In Jesus' name, I pray. Amen.

34

More Life Prepared for Us

From living by faith in Christ, let us follow the design to the conclusion of what it means to LIVE beyond a mere Christianity.

Live by the Living Word

"Deal bountifully with thy servant, that I may **live**, and keep thy word." Psalm 119:17

"The righteousness of thy testimonies is everlasting: give me understanding, and I shall live. Psalm 119:144

"But he answered and said, It is written, Man shall not **live** by bread alone, but by every word that proceedeth out of the mouth of God." Matthew 4:4

> **"Being born again, not of corruptible seed,
> but of incorruptible, by the word of God,
> which liveth and abideth for ever."**
> 1 Peter 1:23

Live in Christ

"For the Son of man is not come to destroy men's **live**s, but to save them." Luke 9:56

"Verily, verily, I say unto you, The hour is coming, and now is, when the dead shall hear the voice of the Son of God: and they that hear shall **live**." John 5:25

"I am the living bread which came down from heaven: if any man eat of this bread, he shall **live** for ever: and the bread that I will give is my flesh, which I will give for the life of the world." John 6:51

"And whosoever **live**th and believeth in me shall never die. Believest thou this?" John 11:26

"For in him we **live**, and move, and have our being; as certain also of your own poets have said, For we are also his offspring." Acts 17:28

"For whether we **live**, we **live** unto the Lord; and whether we die, we die unto the Lord: whether we **live** therefore, or die, we are the Lord's." Romans 14:8

"And that he died for all, that they which **live** should not henceforth live unto themselves, but unto him which died for them, and rose again." 2 Corinthians 5:15

"For though he was crucified through weakness, yet he **live**th by the power of God. For we also are weak in him, but we shall **live** with him by the power of God toward you." 2 Corinthians 13:4

More Life Prepared for Us

"I am crucified with Christ: nevertheless I **live**; yet not I, but Christ **live**th in me: and the life which I now **live** in the flesh I **live** by the faith of the Son of God, who loved me, and gave himself for me." Galatians 2:20

> "Who died for us, that, whether we wake or sleep,
> we should live together with him."
> 1 Thessalonians 5:10

"It is a **faith**ful saying: For if we be dead with him, we shall also **live** with him:" 2 Timothy 2:11

"Ye also, as **live**ly stones, are built up a spiritual house, an holy priesthood, to offer up spiritual sacrifices, acceptable to God by Jesus Christ." 1 Peter 2:5

"In this was manifested the love of God toward us, because that God sent his only begotten Son into the world, that we might **live** through him." 1 John 4:9

Live in the Spirit

> "It is the spirit that quickeneth;
> the flesh profiteth nothing:
> the words that I speak unto you,
> they are spirit, and they are life."
> John 6:63

"For if ye **live** after the flesh, ye shall die: but if ye through the Spirit do mortify the deeds of the body, ye shall **live**." Romans 8:13

"If we **live** in the Spirit, let us also walk in the Spirit. Galatians 5:25

"Furthermore we have had fathers of our flesh which corrected us, and we gave them reverence: shall we not much rather be in subjection unto the Father of spirits, and **live**?" Hebrews 12:9

Live in Peace

"If it be possible, as much as lieth in you, **live** peaceably with all men." Romans 12:18

> "Finally, brethren, farewell.
> Be perfect, be of good comfort,
> be of one mind, live in peace;
> and the God of love and peace shall be with you."
> 2 Corinthians 13:11

Live Godly

"Teaching us that, denying ungodliness and worldly lusts, we should **live** soberly, righteously, and godly, in this present world;" Titus 2:12

"Who his own self bare our sins in his own body on the tree, that we, being dead to sins, should **live** unto righteousness: by whose stripes ye were healed." 1 Peter 2:24"

> "That he no longer should live the rest of his time
> in the flesh to the lusts of men,
> but to the will of God."
> 1 Peter 4:2

"Yea, and all that will **live** godly in Christ Jesus shall suffer persecution." 2 Timothy 3:12

Live Sacrificially

"**Men hazarded their lives for the name of our Lord Jesus Christ.**" (Acts 15:26).

"Fear none of those things which thou shalt suffer: behold, the devil shall cast some of you into prison, that ye may be tried; and ye shall have tribulation ten days: be thou **faith**ful unto death, and I will give thee a **crown of life**." Revelation 2:10

> "And they overcame him
> by the blood of the Lamb,
> and by the word of their testimony;
> and they loved not their lives unto the death."
> Revelation 12:11

Dear Father in Heaven, how can we with mere words thank you for who and what you are to us. Enable us to give ourselves willingly, gratefully, prayerfully and humbly to live as you have planned for us. Let us not be satisfied with a mere taste of your grace but fill us with your fulness, the fulness of your Spirit and the fulness of Christ, who in us is no mere hope but the hope of glory— eternity, here, now, and forever with you. In Jesus' name, we thank you and praise you. Amen.

35

Conclusion to a *mere* Christianity

In this conclusion, I hope to put to rest the idea that there is such a thing as a *mere* Christianity. The Christian faith is simple but profound; enough but much more than we can know.

Our God and Father, the Creator and Redeemer of His people, did not bring the world into existence by a mere pittance of His grace. He did not send His only begotten Son into the world to provide only a possibility for salvation nor was His death upon the cross a means to provide only a pitiful life here on earth.

God, before the foundation of the world, planned to bless His people in Christ with *every spiritual blessing in the heavenly places* (Ephesians 1:3-4).

King Ahasuerus offered Queen Esther half his kingdom; so did King Herod offer to the daughter of Herodias (Esther 5:3; Mark 6:23).

In the Sermon on the Mount Jesus said, "Blessed are the poor in spirit, for theirs is the kingdom of God (Matthew 5:3). He told His disciples, "It is the Father's pleasure to give you the kingdom" (Luke 12:32). He promises to share His kingdom and His glory with all His children.

God does not offer us a bare existence as a follower of Christ, but the promise that we are new creatures with an *inheritance, incorruptible, undefiled, reserved in heaven for us who are kept by the power of God until His appearing* (1 Peter 1:7).

In this book, I have referenced books by C. S. Lewis, Francis Schaeffer, and Oswald Chambers with points of what they wrote in the past and one sermon by Jonathan Edwards—all to encourage further personal study and gleaning of God's Word.

If we take seriously what is written in the previous chapters of this book, we see the makings of the Holy Spirit's work in the hearts and lives of men. We have written of the truth that there is no status quo to Christianity. While some may experience a low profile of faith, others are called to live sacrificially.

Either of these requires the supernatural power and presence of God to change the hearts of men.

In our references, we see the life Christ came to give. It is an abundant life (John 10:10) beginning here and now that transitions us from this life into the next. Those who have this life in Christ are willing to die for His name's sake to keep this life forever.

Though this is the conclusion (except for testimonies by two other witnesses), this series will never end. God's Grace ~ God's Glory will continually be a platform for proclaiming the legacy of His kingdom as long as the Lord wills.

> "Because strait is the gate, and narrow is the way,
> which leadeth unto life,
> and few there be that find it."
> Matthew 7:14

36
Unshakable Hope

Bill Sweeney is a well-known blogger on WordPress. I share His witness that Christ has made him an arrow in His quiver. His testimony is one that proves life beyond a mere Christianity. Bill is a witness of God's working when his life was shaken and turned upside down. Before his sudden diagnosis of ALS, he would have been a witness for Christ but not to the degree that he is now. A mere Christianity would not have been enough to bring him through the last twenty-three years. We praise the Lord for the work He continues to do in Bill and his family. You can follow his blog **Unshakable Hope.com**. We share a synopsis of his story in this chapter. Even as this book is being published, he is battling a respiratory infection, perhaps pneumonia, again.

"In late October 1996, just weeks after my 36th birthday, I was diagnosed with a terminal disease called **Amyotrophic Lateral Sclerosis.** After hearing the long and difficult-to-pronounce name, I understood why people use the abbreviation of ALS or call it "Lou Gehrig's Disease" (after the famous New York Yankees' player that died from it.)

The diagnosis—that I had 2 to 5 years to live—came as a shock because I had always enjoyed such great health. I didn't even have a family doctor and had never spent one day in a hospital. Our 11-year-marriage was great and our daughters (ages 7 & 4) were healthy and happy.

A few years earlier, we had built a new home and I had been promoted to the regional sales manager position that I had wanted for 10 years.

Every aspect of our lives was working well; we were living our small part of the *American Dream*.
I quickly discovered that trials don't just affect one area; a health crisis impacts the financial, emotional and spiritual areas, as well as relationships. One part is connected to others like parts of an engine. When one breaks, it affects the performance of the whole engine.

Within a year of being diagnosed, I could no longer walk or talk, so I had to resign my job.

Even though ALS has drastically changed my life and that of my wife and our two daughters, I don't believe anyone should allow a disease or any life-challenge to define who we are. To do so is to give that challenge more credit than it deserves and is the first step on a dead-end road of hopelessness.

This trial has taught us that the only way to experience genuine and consistent hope, peace, and joy in the middle of a trial is to view our lives and situations through God's eyes. For me, learning this was a long and difficult process—but a rewarding one; an ongoing process that will continue until the day I go to be with the Lord.

Starting a Blog
I started my blog *Unshakable Hope.com* as a means to pass along some lessons I've learned through the course of this trial and hopefully to help others avoid some detrimental (hope-stealing) mistakes I made.

I am writing a book to share more of what the Lord was been doing in our lives. It is truly more than what we may see as a mere Christianity—beyond anything we could have imagined.

These are important lessons for everyone to learn. I heard someone say, "If you're not going through a trial now, you can expect one." That is not what anyone would call "good news," but it is the truth.

We don't have to fear trials because God can handle anything this life brings our way, and with His help, we can endure as we see all things through the eyes of Christ!

The Reason for our Trials
I don't believe God causes trials, but He clearly allows them for reasons we will never fully understand in this life. Whatever reasons God has for them, He has accomplished two major things for me: He helped me reset my priorities and form my character.

God Helps us Reset our Priorities
It is from the following references that I chose the name *Unshakable Hope* as a title for my ministry.

> **"And this word, Yet once more, signifieth the removing of those things that are shaken, as of things that are made, that those things which cannot be shaken may remain. Wherefore we receiving a kingdom which cannot be moved, let us have grace, whereby we may serve God acceptably with reverence and godly fear."** Hebrews 12:27-28

I discovered that prior to this trial, I was unknowingly putting my faith in my health, finances, and many other things that have been shaken.

God Forms Our Character

Through the years and His shaping process, I continue to experience hope as one thing that cannot be shaken; and so, I have witnessed this *Unshakable Hope*."

> "And not only so, but we glory in tribulations also; knowing that tribulation worketh patience; And patience experience: and experience, hope; And hope maketh not ashamed; because the love of God is shed abroad in our hearts by the Holy Ghost which is given unto us." Romans 5:3-5

Bill

(Gracious Father in heaven, who has planned our eternity with you, I thank you for Bill and others who can witness of faith and unshakable hope in you. You are the giver of true life in Christ to all your children as you bring us through the trials and circumstances of this life. In Jesus' name, I praise you. Amen.)

37

Everything for His Glory and our Good

Terri and Bill were friends through WordPress before I knew them. I met Terri through Bill's blog. After reading her first post, I knew they both had the same unique witness of a relationship with our Lord Jesu Christ. Talking to her, sharing our blogs and emails, were the Lord's means of leading me to ask for her contribution, which is included in this chapter. She has been a blessing to me as I have seen the Lord's working in her life. Here is her condensed story.

"It is always a privilege to share how God delivered me from an ongoing struggle with addiction.

Before 2013, I was looking for self-worth through things of this world. Now that I have none of these, I am reliant on God for peace and completeness. On a bright August afternoon after fervent prayer, seeking a closer relationship with Him, I was getting something to eat. Dizziness caused me to fall, snapping the C3 vertebrae of my neck. I was paralyzed without communication with the outside world for almost two days. After spending much time in the hospital, I now live as a quadriplegic in a nursing facility.

> "And we know that all things work together for good to them that love God, to them who are the called according to his purpose." Romans 8:28

With all the emotions I've experienced over the last six years, and all the trials I've endured, I know it was all part of a plan to teach me, to mold me, and to keep me faithful through the remainder of this life. These circumstances have brought me to a deep, meaningful relationship with God and abiding relationships with others. Today I would rather be depressed, knowing God is with me than to return to my former life.

> "Although the fig tree shall not blossom, neither shall fruit be in the vines; the labour of the olive shall fail, and the fields shall yield no meat; the flock shall be cut off from the fold, and there shall be no herd in the stalls: Yet I will rejoice in the Lord, I will joy in the God of my salvation." Habakkuk 3:17-18

Apart from Him, I have no good thing. I still suffer emotionally and physically, but I am joyful in the richness of God. What I have learned from prayer, intense Bible study, and input from biblical scholars, is that God is in control of my life. He knows what he is doing. He loves me. And He is good.

A Soldier of the Cross

A soldier of the cross does not live by his feelings. We endure for the promise of a harvest of righteousness. When we trust God in the hardest of times, He renews our strength and enables us to soar in our relationship with him. It is not easy, but the longer we persevere, the more we grow and bear much fruit for His kingdom.

"For which cause we faint not; but though our outward man perish, yet the inward man is renewed day by day. For our light affliction, which is but for a moment, worketh for us a far more exceeding and eternal weight of glory;
While we look not at the things which are seen, but at the things which are not seen: for the things which are seen are temporal; but the things which are not seen are eternal." 2 Corinthians 4:16-18

As I fix my eyes upward, my troubles seem *light and momentary*. I continue to run with perseverance the race God has marked out for me. Through my blog, **Diary of a Quadriplegic,com,** many are praying and encouraging me, and they are encouraged with how God has been working in my life.

The old is gone, and the new has begun.

I have a bright future ahead, even as God enables me to mentor other spinal cord injury patients.

What we see as hopeless in this world, God sees as opportunities to glorify himself."

Terri

A CLOSING PRAYER

(Dear Gracious Father, I have ended this treatise with the testimonies of two of your precious children. They witness of your presence and power in the worst of times on this earth. By the same blessedness you have given me by knowing Bill and Terri, I pray you would bless others. By your Holy Spirit, draw to your Holy Word those who will be witnesses of your grace, your goodness, and your glory. Let us look beyond this world and the teachings of finite men to the open gates of heaven where you wait to pour out your love and your mercy upon us here, now, and forever. In Jesus' name, I pray. Amen.)
Fran

From the Author

Ten years after thinking my life was coming to an end, God is still working to reveal Himself to me. In my eightieth year, the new heart He gave me twenty-seven years ago is continually filled and overflowing with His grace. It is through the power of His will that He has enabled me to live joyfully as a caregiver for members of our family: my father with cancer, my grandchildren, my mother with dementia, and my husband, who is an amputee with heart disease and diabetes. There is no better life than that of serving the Master by serving others.

We began writing these wonderful things of His kingdom so as to provide a legacy for our grandchildren. From file boxes to computer documents, we have been creating an archive by publishing our books since 2016, so these will be available to future generations. They are here for anyone who wants to read of how the Lord works in the hearts and lives of His people as He is preparing us to share His eternal glory. Profits from sales of our books are designated for missions and charity.
Fran

"For the Lord is good, His mercy is everlasting, and His truth endures to all generations." Psalm 100:5

FREE EBook
FIRST THINGS That Last FOREVER
And
Other books by Fran Rogers on Amazon.com.

Blog: godsgracegodsglory.com
Facebook: Father and Family Books
Contact: f.rogers@bellsouth.net

Little Books About the Magnitude of God *(Published*)*

*FIRST THINGS That Last FOREVER
*TWO FULL PLATES ~ Learning to be a Caregiver
*The Garden of GOD'S WORD~ **The Purpose and Delight of BIBLE STUDY**
*The LITTLE BOAT
and other Short Stories of GOD'S GRACE
*GOD Is Our Goal
Notes on Paul's Letter to the Romans
Legacy of the Seven Psalms + One
God's Grace ~ God's Glory

Series What the Holy Bible Says

*What the Holy BIBLE Says About LIGHT
*What the Holy BIBLE Says About the WORD of GOD
What the Holy BIBLE Says About LIFE

Other Books

*Prayers That Bring the House Down
*One Month to Live ~ A Father's Last Words
*A Broad Review of Andrew Murray's Humility"
*Child Keeping ~ God's Blessing to Parents
Waiting is Not a Game ~ Articles of Faith
The Master Gardener and other Poems of GOD'S GRACE

www.ingramcontent.com/pod-product-compliance
Lightning Source LLC
Chambersburg PA
CBHW022356040426
42450CB00005B/202